BROKEN FOR A PURPOSE

BROKEN
FOR A
Purpose

Gisela Yohannan

BOOKS

a division of Gospel for Asia
www.gfa.org

Broken for a Purpose

ISBN: 1-59589-000-9

Published by gfa books, a division of Gospel for Asia
1800 Golden Trail Court
Carrollton, TX 75010 USA
Phone: (972) 300-7777
Fax: (972) 300-7778

Printed in the United States of America

For more information about other materials, visit our website: www.gfa.org.

TABLE OF CONTENTS

INTRODUCTION

As we walk through this life on earth, we are faced outwardly with many hardships, difficulties, sometimes poverty and even persecution. Yet there are other struggles and battles that are often much more intense, much more painful and much more severe than these.

These are the battles we face on the inside, the ones that take place in our hearts. So often no one knows about them and no one cares. At times, we are not able to share them with anyone. We fight lonely, frightened and desperate. The Lord's answers and interventions seem so far away. We know that the outcome of some of these battles will determine if we make it or break under them.

Yet when victory arrives and we have overcome, the effect on our own life and the lives of others is tremendous: We have been broken for a purpose!

This book talks about some of these inward struggles. As you read it, may the Lord encourage you to trust Him as He leads you through your "valleys of the shadow of death" to victory.

—Gisela Yohannan

1. To Build A Life

"Lord, why do You lead me through such painful experiences to learn a certain spiritual truth? Do You have to let me taste such difficulty and so much hurt just to understand You? Couldn't You have done it an easier way?"

I was sitting on my bed, thinking about the months past, in one way grateful for the things I learned, in another wondering why God chose such a hard way. I was not complaining, just asking the One who I know loves me the most.

Very lovingly, the Lord explained His reason to me that afternoon.

When a teacher is standing in front of a classroom and lectures, the students will at best keep part of his lecture in their minds; the rest might be in their notebooks. For the exam, the students will learn their notes by heart, so they will be able to recite the correct answers. Yet if you ask them 5 or 10 years later about the same lesson, they probably will have forgotten 95 percent of it.

The Holy Spirit is our Teacher. His job is *not* to give us some classroom lectures on holiness, worship and righteousness, but *to build our lives*. It takes more than a lecture to shape our whole being into the image of Christ! This is God's ultimate purpose for every believer.

There are, of course, many different teaching methods. Yet the most lasting, but painful, way of learning is by experience. A child will remember for the rest of his life that fire is hot after he has touched a flame only once. The more difficult an experience, the greater the permanent impact it makes on our lives.

God chose this practical but lasting way of teaching for His own Son: "He learned obedience from the things which He suffered" (Hebrews 5:8).

Jesus selected this type of teaching for His disciples: They spent three years walking with Him, observing His life and learning from each daily situation. Jesus did not hand out preprinted lectures to them. Instead, He used normal events, circumstances and difficulties to teach them spiritual truth by experience, which resulted in completely changed hearts.

The Holy Spirit chooses the same practical approach for us as well. He knows our human frame, our forgetfulness, our distant, insensitive heart toward the spiritual world, our darkened understanding and our inability to convert spiritual truth into practical, everyday life.

When the Holy Spirit accepted His job as our Teacher, He looked very carefully at each of us, and then He designed an individual curriculum for every born-again, redeemed person.

When He put my textbook together, He considered my ability to learn, my life span, my weaknesses, my fears, my background, my culture, my former lifestyle and the plan God has for me as a believer. In my textbook, He included all the aspects of the nature of Jesus.

So when the Holy Spirit guides me through the many lessons and at the end of my life completes the last page of my textbook with me, I should have come to the fullness and maturity of Christ. I should now look like Him.

When the Lord saved us, He gave us His joy, peace, assurance of salvation and eternal life. But somehow in our minds, we often expect God to remove all the difficulties and hardships of our life from now on, so as believers we can enjoy an easier, more comfortable life than the rest of mankind. But Jesus did not make such a promise. He only promised to be with us always. In fact, He told us in advance that we would suffer persecution and trials—as He did—if we are to become His disciples.

This actually means that aside from the difficulties a "natural" (unsaved) person faces, we will be in a continuous spiritual battle, one that is not against flesh and blood. Yet in the midst of all of this, Jesus assures us of peace that is not of this world and power that enables us to be more than conquerors.

So the Holy Spirit does not have to create extra-good or extra-terrible circumstances to teach me lessons. But in His wisdom He carefully uses everything that comes along the road of my life, as well as the spiritual battles in which I am involved, as lessons designed just for me, to conform me closer to the image of Christ.

If I understand this truth and daily, consciously remember it, I will learn to view my trials, disappointments, persecutions and victories as opportunities for the Holy Spirit to build and mold my life.

Then, even during the most difficult and painful times in my life that strip me of all that I thought I was, I will be able to say, "Yes, Lord," trusting Him, knowing He is bringing me at that moment one step closer to look like Him.

But why should the Holy Spirit go through all this trouble to try to change me so entirely? Why can't He be satisfied with my salvation?

The Bible declares that soon a day will be coming, after we have finished our life on earth, when Jesus wants to present us before His Father.

On that day, He will take my hand in His and lead me before the throne of God. Jesus will then testify before the Father and all the angels of heaven that I am bought by His blood and that I am His workmanship, completed, lacking nothing, truly a part of Him—His body.

It will be the most precious time ever when my Savior confesses me before His Father and all of heaven. How thankful I will be at that moment for my Teacher, the Holy Spirit, and for every lesson in my textbook.

That day I will stand before the throne of God, not only washed by the blood of the Lamb but also clothed with Christ's righteousness and His very nature, which make me totally acceptable to the Father. I will look at my Lord and realize the greatness of His love for me, to allow me to go through painful teaching so I can share the glory of His nature for all eternity.

2. BEYOND FORGIVENESS

Until a few days ago, I thought I didn't have a problem with forgiveness.

In fact, I felt I had more willingness to forgive than most other Christians I knew. Since the time I was saved, there had been plenty of opportunities to forgive, and some of them were not at all easy!

This week as I reviewed the most recent incident, which I felt was the hardest of them all, I discovered that my concept of forgiveness was lacking something.

Yes, so far I had forgiven everyone who ever had done wrong to me, and I had even asked some people to forgive me if I failed them unknowingly, just to make sure my walk with the Lord was clear.

This time, also, I had forgiven—without it being asked of me—and I had asked forgiveness for any hurt I might have caused, even though I did not feel I had done wrong. I had not received any response or apology, and the person did not seem to recognize any wrong in his own actions. In fact, I saw more pride afterward than before. Yet these results had no effect on me and did not bother me. Maybe it will take years, who knows, for that person to see or admit his wrong. I am not waiting or expecting, now or later, for any better results. All I want is to be able to serve the Lord with all my heart and a clear conscience.

I felt the hurt in my heart longer than any other time, and the remembrance is still somewhat painful. Yet God has taken care of all that, and I am grateful to acknowledge His strength and thank Him for the lessons I learned.

MORE THAN FORGIVING

But two days ago, the Lord reminded me of a Bible verse I had known almost all my life. Because it would not leave my mind, I decided to take my Bible and read the whole passage so I wouldn't miss anything. Each of Jesus' statements in that chapter seemed so powerful, so impossible to live out or achieve with human strength. But none of them bothered me until I came to verse 44 in Matthew 5, the very verse I had thought about for the past two days: "Love your enemies."

This bothered me, because I realized that I never had made much of a connection between forgiving someone and loving my enemy. As far as I could remember, I had never called anyone my "enemy." But this time I realized that the Lord wanted to tell me that my "enemy" whom I was supposed to love was actually the same person I had forgiven.

For me, forgiveness ended when I no longer held

something against that person. My highest form of forgiveness was to forgive without it being asked of me and to make the first step, even if the other person was at fault. Now I realized that there was more *beyond* that!

I discovered that the completion of forgiveness was to "love your enemy." What was more, I was not living it, especially not in this last encounter.

Whenever I forgave my husband, my children or a friend, it didn't seem difficult to love them. In fact, I had a desire to be close to them and show them extra love and compassion, hoping they wouldn't feel so low after they failed me. But this situation was different. I couldn't find any desire in me to ever want to get close to this person, let alone love him.

Yet as I thought of this command to "love your enemy," I also had to admit that it sounded like it was meant to be very practical, not an abstract philosophical idea. Also, I saw clearly that there were no exceptions or distinctions between "easy-to-love" and "hard-to-love" enemies.

What was I to do with what I discovered? First, I thought, I would see how Jesus dealt with it.

How Much Does Jesus Love His Enemy?

Jesus was always very practical with biblical truth. He lived it so literally that people could observe with their own eyes what He meant when He said something.

Let us see how Jesus interpreted "love your enemy."

Actually, Jesus had many enemies, but He allowed His most "deadly" one to live with Him. This was not because Jesus didn't recognize who he was. John 2:25 says, "He did not need anyone to bear witness concerning man for He Himself knew what was in man."

For three years, Judas walked with Him on the road, ate with Him and slept on the same floor. Jesus taught him just the same as the other disciples, provided for his needs and allowed him to be part of every event, miracle, struggle, prayer meeting and teaching session. He even gave Judas power to heal the sick and to preach.

Every day, Judas was able to talk with Jesus, to see Him and take up His time.

When he finally came to betray Him, Jesus called him "My friend." Jesus meant "friend" with His whole heart, because He didn't use vain words. He actually loved Judas, knowing from the very beginning what Judas was going to do three years later.

There is not one report in the Gospels that Jesus treated Judas differently, put him down or loved him less than the other disciples. All the time Jesus knew Judas' heart, yet He showed him love, expecting one day that he would pierce and crush His emotions — which were as human as mine.

I believe that if Judas would not have killed himself, Jesus would have had enough love to offer forgiveness to him after His resurrection. After all, He forgave Peter, who denied Him three times in a row.

From this relationship, I can see that Jesus' love was totally a supernatural one, impossible for me to produce in my heart. It's just not there. I had thought that my forgiveness was above average. But God did not ask me to evaluate something by what I had achieved, but by what Jesus said and portrayed in His life. Looking at this, I had to confess that my ability to forgive was far below His. In fact, I was almost afraid to honestly evaluate it to see how much lower it was.

How Much Do I Love My Enemy?

I forgave for Christ's sake.

I didn't ask God—anymore—to pay him back with the same hurt or to punish him. I even asked God to bless his life.

I didn't expect or ask for any apology, and I did not expect him to admit his wrong, then or in the future.

I talked to him, even though I didn't really know what to say. I smiled—at least sometimes, offered food, gave him a place to sleep when he came to our home and occasionally visited his family.

Yet I didn't want any closeness. I didn't want to receive anything from him—even though I accepted it because I didn't want to make him feel bad and as a believer I knew it would be wrong. In my heart, I wished to be left alone and not to see that person—at least not often. I tolerated his presence, even if it reminded me of my hurt.

There was no bitterness in my heart, no hate, no anger . . . but also no love.

Even if I wanted to love that person, it was totally above my strength, above my ability, above anything I could find in my heart. With all honesty I could say *I didn't even want to love that person.*

I Stopped along the Way

God always looks for completeness in anything He does. So one-half or two-thirds forgiveness will not be sufficient in His eyes. His goal is that, like Jesus, I should offer complete forgiveness: "Love your enemy!"

It was as though I was on a journey in life, with a specific destination to reach: complete forgiveness. Looking at Jesus, my example, I realized that I never reached my goal—I had stopped along the way!

When we are treated wrongly, or we think we are, as humans we will all go through a time of difficult emotional hurt. Yet as believers, we should be able to walk through all these stages with Christ's help and end up with complete forgiveness in our hearts, restored fellowship (if at all possible) and even love for our enemy.

If the outcome is less than this, we have never reached our destination! That discovery convicted me, because I found I didn't even want to love my enemy!

By now, the question became not what this person did or whether I had evaluated all his actions correctly. All of a sudden it became a matter of my heart's attitude toward God.

Why Do I Have Trouble to Even Consider Loving My Enemy?

If God shows me a truth and I am not able to accept it or to live it, then He expects me to check my heart. There must be something that sets me apart from His nature, something that needs to be identified and dealt with. *For a child of God, there should be nothing that resists God's Spirit!*

I discovered that my problem was *fear:*

- Fear of hurting again.

- Fear of finding out more than I already knew. I forgave what I personally saw and heard. But suppose that there was more said or done than I knew of. If that person had the courage to treat me this way right to my face, what about behind my back? If I came to know *all,* would my hurt start over again? Would my forgiveness still stand, or would it crumble to nothing?

- Fear of new hurt. What if that person didn't really change his heart, was only pretending and took advantage of the situation later?

- Fear of sharing myself, letting someone come close who could once again crush me.

I AM HIS WORKMANSHIP!

After I understood that there was more beyond forgiveness than what I had practiced and after I had identified my problem, I found that I still wasn't able to love my enemy!

I sincerely prayed, and I cried. I cried not because I wasn't able to love that person, but because I wasn't able to obey the Lord. My desire was to walk with Jesus and to do His will. But even after I spent time in prayer, I couldn't find or produce any love in my heart to give to my "enemy" — all I could find was tolerance.

That afternoon, while reading a chapter in a Christian book, I came across some references that made me forget everything else I had just read. These verses were the answer to my "love your enemy" problem:

"For we are His workmanship . . ." (Ephesians 2:10).

"For it is God who is at work in you, both to will and to work for His good pleasure" (Philippians 2:13).

"Greater is He who is in you than he who is in the world" (1 John 4:4).

Because I am *His,* not my own, workmanship, it will be His goal to complete what is lacking in me. Therefore, it must also have been His desire to show me my inability to love my enemy.

Furthermore, if He is the One who is producing the "willingness" and the "working," then I can stop trying to come up with a solution myself.

The Bible tells me that *He is able to create something out of nothing, just as He did the universe.* So even if there is nothing in my heart, He can create what is missing!

I realized that I needed to trust Him, knowing that He is able to complete the work He started in me! Because He is greater than my own heart, my enemy and even Satan, His work will always be an absolute success.

Praise God, I didn't know how, but I could see that there was victory for me.

I had found the answer to my incapability to obey the Lord. Once again that afternoon, I knelt down to pray, confessing my inability to love and giving myself into His loving hands to work on my heart.

This is what I prayed:

> Lord, I want to obey You and love my enemy, but I can't even make my heart want to. Today I am not able to imagine how I could ever succeed. But You told me that I am Your workmanship. Today I submit to You to start working on me, and I trust You to create the willingness in my heart and the ability to love.
>
> Most of all, I need Your presence. From other difficult times in my life, I know that in Your presence all the things of this earth become small; and I know my fear of hurting, my wounded memories and my unwillingness will melt away and make room for Your love that is greater than I.
>
> Thank You for starting to work on me from this moment on.

From the lines above, you can see that I have shared my heart with you. I have allowed you to see my hurt, my inability to love, my unwillingness, my fear and what God has taught me. At first I thought it would be too personal and too embarrassing to write all this for you to read. But I believe God wants me to allow you to see my own struggle.

Maybe you also have an enemy you can't love! You might not call him an "enemy." It might be even your wife, your husband, your child, your father or mother, your best friend, your fellow Christian or your pastor who has hurt you in such a way that you can't find any desire or will-ingness in your heart to love him again. You have forgiven, but your forgiveness is incomplete. You have never quite reached that "destination" of loving your enemy.

I want to invite you to pray with all your heart the kind of prayer I prayed, trusting the Lord to create in you the willingness and the ability to love that person as He would. By faith you can know today that there is victory for you, because "the things impossible with men are possible with God" (Luke 18:27).

Epilogue

When I first wrote this chapter, I was wondering what would happen if someone who read this book asked me directly if my prayer worked and my heart really changed. After all, I wrote this chapter in the middle of my struggle, and not enough time had passed yet to see if it were true — that the Lord could not only change a heart, but actually create something that was not there previously.

Since I wrote these pages, more than a year has passed. The Lord was faithful; He has not only healed my hurt, but He has definitely created something in my heart that was not there before: a willingness to love my "enemy." I am still cautious in my approach. But I feel as though the Lord has literally taken my hand and is walking with me step-by-step to reach the goal He has set before me. My fear, too, has grown smaller and smaller; at the same time, my trust in the Lord has increased.

A few weeks ago, I talked to the Lord about the change He brought into my heart. I felt He was telling me that through this trial, He has given me an opportunity in my life to deliberately choose to be like Him. I could hate or be indifferent to that person for the rest of my life, or I could love the same as Jesus would love.

Today there is much joy in my heart. Truly Jesus is able to give us the power to be His sons and daughters, not in words only but also in deeds.

3. HOW MUCH VALUE DO I HAVE?

It was past midnight, and I was lying on my bed, unable to sleep.

I was thinking about the experience I had gone through today. The people whom I had been so sure would give value for my life had reacted totally opposite of my expectations.

They were the ones who should know my heart and be able to see what was motivating me to give up my own way of life to serve the Lord and those to whom He had sent me.

Today there had been a meeting, and there was also a "talk" about me. But to my surprise, the things I thought I had done well were not even mentioned, and all my efforts were overlooked.

When all was concluded, they only listed the things I had not been able to achieve—at least not yet. In fact, all during the meeting, the only thing I heard about myself was criticism. Before the meeting ended, I was told that however I might try, I would never meet their standard of performance.

I knew I had done my best, not perfect but better than I had hoped for. It would have encouraged me greatly to try even harder if someone would have acknowledged just one thing I had done well. It surely would have put a smile on my face and joy in my heart. What was most difficult to accept was that I had acted out of love toward the Lord and toward them with my efforts, and they had not seen this at all.

Now I was presented with the cold fact that all my hard work to prove my willingness and my love obviously meant nothing!

A storm was raging outside. I could hear the thunder and see the lightning flashing over the dark sky. The rain was pouring down, and the trees were shaking in the wind.

I felt so low. Tears ran down my face. The people who I thought knew me, whom I had loved, had not understood my heart. It seemed as if none of them valued my life very much.

Was all I had done for nothing—the price I had paid and the love I had shown?

I had not waited for any recognition or reward, just an acknowledgment of my attempts and perhaps of my love.

Slowly the hours of the night were passing by, and I turned from one side of the bed to the other without finding any sleep.

Would I have enough courage tomorrow morning to get up and again serve others with all my heart, again try to love and give up my life? I didn't think it was hurt pride that I felt, but rather deep discouragement. My self-worth had sunk to zero.

If those who knew me didn't value my life, who else would, I wondered? As soon as I had asked this question, I heard the voice of the Lord answering me in my heart:

"*I* value your life. Look at the cross; you mean that much to Me!"

All of a sudden my heart became very quiet, and for a long time I lay on my bed thinking about the cross:

- How much it cost Jesus to go there!

- How much hardship He faced to live and walk as a man on this earth!

- How shameful it was to carry that cross on His back through Jerusalem, up to the hill of Golgotha!

- How extremely difficult it must have been for Him, who knew no sin, to bear mine!

- How painful it was to willingly allow the soldiers to drive those nails through His hands and feet!

- How hard it must have been for Him to listen to the mocking of the crowd!

- How lonely and rejected He felt when God His Father turned His face away from Him!

- How much He suffered hanging on this cross, waiting hour after hour for death to come!

All that . . . because He valued my life that much!

Looking at the cross, I felt the deep love of Jesus that He has for me. Suddenly it didn't matter anymore that the people I knew and loved had not valued me or the things I did.

It was early in the morning when I fell asleep. The storm was still raging outside, but my heart had found comfort in the knowledge of the cross and the value the Son of God had given to my life.

4. WHO AM I?

A few years ago we traveled by train to Tamil Nadu. The children and I were especially excited to see so much of the countryside and to learn about the people and the Gospel work in this state.

Of course, we had fun eating the *wodas*, bananas and oranges the local people were selling at every train stop, and I believe Daniel and Sarah took advantage of drinking more *chaia* than they were allowed at home!

Because our train ride was overnight, I had time to read my Bible and to think about the Lord's work.

The Lord had been very gracious to me and had given me many opportunities to give my testimony, to share in meetings, to attend some pastors' conferences and to travel together with my husband to different parts of India. Also, my first book had just come out in the Malayalam language. At that moment I was on the way to visit a mission field, and the next day I was supposed to lay the foundation stone for the first church in that place.

The more I thought of what the Lord allowed me to do and what He was expecting of my life, the more unworthy I felt.

His work was so great and the brothers and sisters I met showed such a dedication and commitment—who was I to encourage them or teach them something?

I started to think of my weaknesses and my failures, about the times I misunderstood others, the times I criticized and judged wrongly (at least in my heart). I remembered well when I was not careful enough to discern and evaluate some people, and they took advantage of my trust and tried to hurt the ministry. Then there were occasions when I was teaching others, and when the test came, I forgot to practice my teaching. How many times had I let the Lord down when He had counted on my boldness, faithfulness and steadfastness?

The more time I spent thinking, the longer the list of my shortcomings seemed to become. Sure, *all* of it was forgiven and covered by grace, yet the remembrance made me feel so unworthy to serve the Lord.

It started to get late in the evening, and we lay down to sleep on the benches in the train. For a long time I prayed, telling the Lord how much I wanted to please Him yet how condemned I felt coming to Him with this background of forgiven failures. That night I asked Him many times, "Lord, who am I that I should do the things You asked me to do?"

By the time I went to sleep, I still didn't feel any better about myself. The question "Who am I?" remained on my heart. It seemed to echo through my mind every time I woke up, when the train stopped and the cries of the peddlers selling *chaia* and *capi* interrupted my sleep. I had told no one about the thoughts I was struggling with, and I only hoped I would somehow feel better the next day.

The next morning I got up quite early. The train was still moving along. Daniel and Sarah were still wrapped in their sheets, trying to open their eyes.

The brother who was traveling with us had been reading his Bible. Afterward, he folded his bedsheet and put it back in his small suitcase. While he was arranging his sheet, he pulled out a small booklet and handed it to me, saying, "I want you to read this. You can keep it."

I took it and looked at the cover page to read the title. There, written in big, bold, red letters, was: "Who Are You?"

I was totally surprised, to say the least. It was almost hard to believe what I was holding in my hand. Only last night I had asked the Lord a hundred times, "Who am I?" and here, as with return mail, I got His answer: "Who Are You?" He surely must love me a great deal to do such a thing!

Quietly I sat on my bench and started reading, curious to see what the Lord had to say to me.

Every page in this booklet exactly described my heart's condition and the thoughts I had struggled with the previous night. The entire message of this booklet was that we live in defeat and self-condemnation as a result of not knowing who we are in Christ Jesus. Then it explained that our rightful position as a believer is the one position in which God Himself sees us: in Jesus!

This means that right now, "by the grace of God I am what I am" (1 Corinthians 15:10):

- I am a son of God (1 John 3:2).

- I am born of God (John 1:13).

- I am an heir of God (Galatians 4:7).

- I am a new creation (2 Corinthians 5:17).

- I am accepted in the Beloved (Ephesians 1:6).

- I am blessed with all spiritual blessings (Ephesians 1:3).

- I am the righteousness of God in Christ Jesus (2 Corinthians 5:21).

- I am free from condemnation (Romans 8:1).

- I am complete in Him (Colossians 2:10).

- I am an overcomer (1 John 4:4).

- I am more than a conqueror (Romans 8:37).

- I am seated with Christ in heavenly places (Ephesians 2:6).

All these declarations sound wonderful, but one look at our Christian lives will tell us that we fall way short in our attempts to live up to them.

How then can God talk about us as if we were already perfect? Because He is all-knowing, He surely must be aware that we fail many times.

You see, God the Father doesn't look at us directly. When He looks at us, He sees us through Jesus. It is just like when I look *through* my kitchen window at the tree in the front yard of our house. I see the tree, but not directly. I see it through the glass of my window. The glass is between me and the tree.

Jesus is just like the glass of my window. He stands between me and God. When God the Father looks at me, He first sees Jesus who is totally holy, righteous and complete. With Him in front of me, my insufficiency is totally covered by the completeness of Jesus.

We must understand that when God calls us a new creation, accepted, the righteousness of God, free from condemnation, a conqueror, complete and so on, He always talks about our *position* as a child of God, *not* about possible perfect deeds.

We received this position when we accepted Jesus as our Savior and Lord. The Bible says that at that moment we were born again and were legally adopted into the family of God. With our position as a true son or daughter of God, we also became heirs together with Jesus.

This means that everything that belongs to Jesus is our inheritance also! All of heaven, eternal life, victory over sin and the devil, righteousness, peace, joy and all the promises in the Bible are ours!

But when will this inheritance go into effect? Five years from now, or when we achieve higher levels of holiness and spirituality, or when we die?

No. Look carefully in your Bible to see how God Himself addresses us and how He talks about our position. Notice that He always uses either past or present tense, never future.

Consider these examples:

- *Now we are* children of God (1 John 3:2).

- You *have been made* complete (Colossians 2:10).

- There *is* therefore *now* no condemnation (Romans 8:1).

Practically, what does this mean?

Right now – I am a new creation. It doesn't matter if I feel like one or not. If I am truly born again, that is what I am. God says so. Maybe it will take a while before others notice it as well, but nevertheless this is what God says I am, and I will declare it thus.

Right now – I am accepted in the Beloved. When I come to the Lord in prayer, I don't have to beg to be accepted. I don't have to work for acceptance, establish my worthiness or present perfect deeds to Him. Before I even knock at His door, God has already declared that I am totally accepted – as I am. I can come joyfully, with confidence, knowing that my Father is already waiting for me and is more than willing to hear my prayer and answer me.

Right now – I am blessed with every spiritual blessing. This means that whatever spiritual blessings God has promised in His Word are mine. He will not withhold them from me. They are not saved up for later. They are mine for today. However, I must remember that He is talking about spiritual blessings, *not* about my selfish, earthly desires and wishes.

Right now — I am the righteousness of God in Christ Jesus. Regardless of my past and my failures, God has forgiven me. Because of Jesus, I *am* the righteousness of God. It doesn't matter how qualified or unqualified I feel.

Right now — I am free from condemnation. God totally forgave me when I came to Him and asked Him to do so. Others may still condemn me. The devil might remind me of my past, and I myself may feel unworthy. But I believe God, and He has declared that at this moment I am free from condemnation.

Right now — I am complete in Him, not because I am perfect in all my deeds but because the completeness of Jesus covers me. He stands between me and God. Only *in Him* I am complete. Apart from Him I am not.

Right now — I am an overcomer and more than a conqueror. The devil tells me that I am a failure, that God cannot use me, that I am weak and that I will never be able to conquer the fear, anger or bad habits I have. The devil is a liar. God has proclaimed that I am an overcomer and am more than a conqueror in all things — no exceptions. Because God said it, I will believe Him and take my place as a child of God. I will walk in His power and in His authority. I know that victory is mine — today.

Right now — I am seated with Christ in heavenly places.
When I look at who I am, I see myself quite differently: I
am in my kitchen cooking food, cleaning floors or washing
clothes. It doesn't look heavenly at all, at least not to me.
But amazingly, God doesn't see me there in the kitchen.
He sees me, at this moment, already sitting with Jesus in
heavenly places.

This truth is totally exciting: He has already watched
me run the race and complete it, and I have won! What an
encouragement for my struggles. The end result of my battle on earth is already established and declared in heaven:
victory — seated with Christ. Praise God.

*I am who God says I am, not who the devil or I myself think I
am.* I must claim, live and confess boldly who I am in Christ;
and I will not only defeat the devil, but I will exercise the
authority and power that is mine together with the position
of being a child of God. Doing so will take all the fear of
unworthiness away, and I will experience the freedom to
come into God's presence knowing I am totally accepted.

Jesus said, "You shall *know* the truth, and the truth shall
make you free" (John 8:32). This means that in my situation,
if I *know* the truth of how God sees me, it will make me free
from condemnation.

How thankful and glad I felt to receive God's answer for
my troubled thoughts. During the remainder of our train
ride I read this booklet twice, and I underlined many para-
graphs in it. I put a date on the cover to remember God's
faithfulness in answering me.

Since then I have read it a number of times. The message has made such a difference in my life!

Strangely, I had read the same Bible verses quoted in that booklet before, but they only had helped me on an "on-and-off" basis. The reason was that I had never knowingly and consciously made them part of my life. This time, God's Word had reached and touched my heart to change it.

I believe the Lord deliberately made such a special event out of this lesson because He saw that I was forgetting it all the time. In His love He planned to teach me in such a practical way to help me remember it forever.

To know who we are in Jesus is not a cheap excuse for our failures, but it is the freedom to serve Him boldly with confidence and with all our hearts.

EPILOGUE

More than a year later, I met this brother again and I told him the story about his booklet. He remembered giving it to me, and he said, "I never gave this booklet to anyone else, before or after. It is good the Lord allows us to serve one another."

5. Sober-Minded Christianity

"What sari shall I wear to church today? I want to wear one you like," I said to my husband, expecting him to pick one. Instead, he said, "Any one, just wear whatever you want."

I insisted, "Tell me the one *you* like; you know, I want to please you."

He looked at me and said jokingly, "This is Western thinking! I settled that 13 years ago when we got married. Why would you want to prove something that doesn't need proving anymore?"

I replied, "I still want to please you as I did 13 years ago." Probably to settle it once and for all, he said, "Wear the one with the orange stripe."

I hurried to get the iron to press out the wrinkles in my sari before I got dressed for church. While I was ironing, I thought about our conversation. I know very well that my husband and most men I can think of don't really like to pick out clothes. Yet I believe that they, as well as everyone else, appreciate when something is done to please them.

But why do people generally think that once a relationship is established, we can forget about doing special things just to please the other person? After a short time, all things that were once special seem to turn into his or her responsibility and duty. Some of the actions remain, but the motivation has totally changed.

HAVE WE LOST OUR SENSITIVE HEART?

When a couple first gets married, the boy and girl are conscious of how they look, how they dress and what they say to one another. They are conscious of how they treat each other's relatives. They try to learn what the other one likes or dislikes. In other words, they are very *sensitive* to please one another.

But if you look at them a few years later, in most cases that sensitivity is gone. They now take each other for granted. They do well as a family, and they fulfill their responsibilities, but they have lost the desire to please each other.

How about when we get a new job in a company? The first day we make sure we are on time, we work as hard as we can, we pay attention to the supervisor and we are polite to our employer. We bring him his tea at break time, and we try to find out as fast as possible what he doesn't like and what pleases him.

What about 2 or 5 or 10 years later? Do we have the same concern to please our employer? Or do we take our job and our boss for granted? We excuse ourselves: "Why should I make extra efforts, why be so punctual, why work so hard, why should I try to please him? My job situation got settled five years ago. No need to take such care to please anymore."

What about our relationship with God? Are we treating God the same way as our marriage partner or our employer?

Think back to when you first got saved! Do you remember how, more than anything else, you wanted to please the Lord? You asked Him about even the smallest details of your life. You only wanted to say what He wanted you to say, to go where it would please Him to have you go and to spend your money in a way that would honor Him. You cried every time you realized you disappointed the Lord with your words or actions. You shared your innermost heart, your most private thoughts with Him. You wanted to include Him in every area of your life, family, home and work.

You searched your Bible for what would please Him and right away started doing the things you found, even at the risk of persecution from your family or community. You wanted to learn more about Him, not to present a speech somewhere but simply to be able to please Him.

How is your relationship to Jesus today, after 5 years of salvation—or 25 years? Are you still the same? Or have you "graduated" to a more "mature" and "sober-minded" Christianity?

Is Our Position Not Enough?

Because our salvation was settled 2, 5, 10 or 22 years ago at our conversion, why should we still do "deeds" to prove we are saved?

The Bible says, "Faith, if it hath not works, is dead" (James 2:17, KJV). The "works" we do make the faith we have in our heart *visible*. Our "actions" prove that our faith is as real as we claim it is.

Abraham had to leave his country before his faith became *visible*. He could have stayed at home and told everyone how much he believed God. No one would have seen the reality of his faith. But his leaving was the proof of the kind of faith that existed in his heart.

In the same way, our love without works is dead. The works we do make the love in our heart *visible*.

If God would have just told us that He loves us, we would have had a difficult time believing it (because we are "hard-to-love" creatures). But God's love became *visible* for everyone when He sent His only Son to die for us.

God doesn't want us to have theory-faith and theory-love. He wants the evidence of what we proclaim we have to be visible and tangible.

We don't do the works to *produce* salvation, faith or love in our hearts. We can't produce this anyway. We do the works because salvation, faith and love are *already* reality in our hearts, and they just become visible by our actions.

It is much like a mango tree. The tree is not growing mangoes to become a mango tree. It produces mangoes *because it already is* a mango tree. But the mango fruit makes visible the kind of tree it is to everyone who looks at it.

For Which Deeds Is the Lord Looking?

"Do the deeds you did at first." This is the advice Jesus gave to the church in Ephesus. He told them in Revelation

2:1–5 that they had left their first love, and He asked them once again to *do the deeds* they did at first.

Actually, they were doing a lot of deeds, and Jesus acknowledged them all:

- Toil
- Perseverance
- Not enduring evil men
- Testing leaders
- Endurance
- Not growing weary
- Hating and not tolerating false doctrines

The deeds they did were all good and necessary to run a church. They did very well in correctly performing their service and ministry. But obviously all this hard work did not count as much in Jesus' eyes as what they had lost.

Please notice that Jesus didn't say, "On what date did you settle your position as a child of God?" He was asking for and expecting deeds.

But what more can He expect from us than being faithful, acting responsibly, keeping all the rules and working hard? He expects "*deeds* of first love"!

WHAT ARE THESE DEEDS OF FIRST LOVE?

We do all the important things: We pray, read the Bible, teach Sunday school, give our offering, have prayer meetings in our home and meet all our church responsibilities, thinking these are the deeds of first love. But we are mistaken.

The real deeds of first love are the very things we did when we first got saved!

These are the things we do for someone just to please that person. They are not the necessary things to maintain a church or a Christian life. They are the "unnecessary" deeds, the unexpected ones, the ones that are not on our timetable. They are the things that we say and do *just for Him* and *just because of Him*. There is no other reason! They are not things that make us famous or bring us profit. They are the deeds we do only for one reason alone, and that is genuine love. We don't expect anything to be paid back—we only want to give of ourselves.

These "first love deeds" are the ones that Jesus says are missing from our lives.

What Is the True Way of Pleasing?

When we lose the sensitivity of our walk with the Lord, we lose the desire to please the Lord just for the sake of pleasing Him, out of pure love for Him.

There are three different types of pleasing. In our society there is a false type of pleasing. We do something for a person out of a selfish desire to gain a profit or to manipulate that person to feel obligated to us.

Then there is a pleasing out of tradition or culture; this looks like the real thing, but it is not from the heart. We find this a lot in our churches and homes. We smile and do things because it fits the image of our denomination or culture to act that way. This type of pleasing is worse than not pleasing at all. It is a living lie.

Finally, there is the true pleasing, the kind Jesus asks from us, the kind that comes from the depths of our heart. This pleasing is the visible evidence of our first love to the Lord.

Did Jesus Do Any Deeds of First Love?

Jesus is our example, not only for obedience and holiness, but also for what it means to do the deeds of first love. He never asks us to live anything He Himself didn't live first.

Jesus maintained His first love to His Father throughout His life on earth. This becomes very clear in His testimony: "And He who sent Me is with Me; He has not left Me alone, for I always do the things that are pleasing to Him" (John 8:29).

He could have said, like us, "My relationship with My Father was settled from eternity past, or on earth at My birth, or baptism; it doesn't need any further proof!" He could have been satisfied in just doing His responsibility. But no, He was doing more—far more! He was always doing the extra things that are pleasing to His Father.

What were some of these extra things?

His longing to be with His Father. We see this longing in Luke 2:49, when He told His earthly parents: "Why is it that you were looking for Me? Did you not know that I had to be in My Father's house?" Also, Luke 5:16 tells us, "But He Himself would often slip away to the wilderness and pray."

His trust in His Father. When Jesus was about to raise Lazarus from the dead, He prayed, "And I knew that Thou

45

hearest Me always" (John 11:42). His prayer displays His total assurance that His Father hears Him and will answer. In Luke 23:46 we read, "Father, into Thy hands I commit My spirit." He prayed this while He was totally separated from God because of our sin.

His total surrender and obedience. These qualities are evident in passages like "My food is to do the will of Him who sent Me, and to accomplish His work" (John 4:34) and "Abba! Father! All things are possible for Thee; remove this cup from Me; yet not what I will, but what Thou wilt" (Mark 14:36).

His compassion, gentleness and love. "And seeing the multitudes, He felt compassion for them, because they were distressed and downcast like sheep without a shepherd" (Matthew 9:36). How many times did He touch those who were sick or spend time talking to someone in need?

As the Son of God, He could have just commanded things to happen, without getting too personally close to the situation and to those sinners, lepers and crippled, sick and demon-possessed people.

But He did the extra things that pleased His Father: He asked them to come to Him, He touched them and showed them extra love. When He was so tired and needed rest, He allowed the women with their children to disturb Him. Instead of getting upset, He blessed them. When a widow was about to bury her only son, we read, "And when the Lord saw her, He felt compassion for her, and said to her, 'Do not weep' " (Luke 7:13).

His forgiveness. For those who crucified Him, He prayed:

"Father forgive them; for they do not know what they are doing" (Luke 23:34). Was it not enough that He was willing to die? No, He was doing the extra things that pleased His Father.

These are just a few examples to help us see that Jesus always did more than His responsibility. He could have healed, performed His acts of duty and then died, without all the "trouble" of these small extra details. But He deliberately chose to be different and continuously find ways to please His Father, whom He loved more than food, comfort and His own life.

THE DIRECT RESULT OF CHRIST'S FIRST LOVE

In John 8:29, Jesus reveals to us the "secret" of His authority to preach and His power to perform miracles, heal the sick, raise the dead and cast out demons: "And He who sent Me *is with Me*; He has not left Me alone."

His secret was *God's presence* with Him every moment of His life. God's presence set Him apart from everyone else, and it made all the difference in His life and ministry.

We know very well that if God's presence is totally with us, we too will be a powerful witness. Many believers can remember times in their lives when it was that way, and God used them mightily. But that was only occasionally, for a few hours, days or weeks.

But *how* did Jesus have God's presence abiding with Him always? Was it easy and automatic for Him because He was God's Son? I don't believe so, because the Bible tells us that He was also just as human as we are. If that is so, did He then do something additional that we have failed to recognize?

Jesus tells us very clearly in this verse that there was a *definite condition in His personal life* that enabled God's presence to be with Him always. Let us read the second part of John 8:29: ". . . for I always do the things that are pleasing to Him."

Jesus' first love relationship to His Father was the condition for God's presence to be with Him. This relationship was evident in deeds, not just in words, traditions, responsibilities or positions. These deeds were purely a continuous, spontaneous expression of His love with the only goal to please His Father.

FIRST LOVE CAN'T BE PRODUCED BY CALCULATION

What about us? We now see the direct connection between first love and God's presence and power. Could we *"use"* our discovery by making the right combination every time we want to achieve great things (for God, of course!)?

Hardly! First love is not something you learn and apply like a formula in mathematics. It is a heart expression! If this love is in our hearts, it will come out in deeds — automatically, without us *making* it happen.

In the same way, the presence and power of God can't be produced by calculation. If we try to do it in this manner, we may fool many people, perhaps even believers. But it will then be the product of the flesh, not of the Spirit. Any result we may achieve with such a "calculated production" will be totally rejected by God.

Just as the gifts of the Spirit *follow* those who believe, in the same way, the presence of God *follows* those whose hearts are completely His. No artificial production is necessary or even possible for either, because they are a direct result of our heart's condition.

GOD IS NOT SATISFIED WITH SUBSTITUTES

Some time ago, I wanted to buy a "Gold Spot" soft drink at a local store. They had run out of it, and they told me they had another product that tasted "just the same." I didn't believe them, but because I was so thirsty I bought it anyway. I was right—this substitute tasted absolutely different. The only similarity with the real thing was the color.

If first love is not in our hearts, the only things that will come out are look-alike substitutes: traditions, good works and fulfilled responsibilities. All these things in themselves might be commendable, but in God's eyes, they are not able to take the place of first love deeds.

CAN OUR LOST RELATIONSHIP BE RESTORED?

But what can we do now if we have lost our sensitive heart toward God, recently or as many as 20, 30 years ago? Is there a way back?

Jesus tells the church of Ephesus *how* to get back. In Revelation 2:5, He says, *"Remember . . . and repent."* This sounds almost harsh for just a "little" offense committed by such a hard-working church. For us it may look like a small thing, yet God takes it so seriously. You know, His heart is deeply wounded when we try to fool Him and substitute our love for Him with great works instead.

To *remember* means to look back at how it was at first, to compare it with now and to recognize the difference. Remembering makes us homesick.

To *repent* means not only admitting we did wrong, but being deeply sorry with all our hearts for our condition. It includes asking for forgiveness and, by God's grace, starting out in the right direction.

How is it possible for our first love to grow again? By spending time in His presence, looking at Him, sharing with Him, remembering what He suffered for us. It is impossible not to learn to love Him again when we truly look into His face.

If you come to Him, not with the hope of becoming powerful but just to please Him once again, He Himself will help you love Him *as you did before*. Jesus would not call us to come back to do the deeds of our first love if He did not know a way to completely restore our relationship with Him. We *must not* be satisfied with a lesser result than "as it was at first."

6. QUALIFIED FOR TESTING

A young Bible school student was talking with me about his plans for his future ministry.

He said, "I am willing to suffer for the Lord." My answer to him was, "Watch out—God is going to test you on this." And the Lord did when He called him to work in Nepal.

EVERYTHING WILL BE TESTED

You may have never said, "I am willing to suffer." But did you say "Amen" at church when your pastor was teaching and explaining some truth from the Bible?

In your prayers, did you ever tell the Lord, "Jesus, I love You more than anyone else. I am willing to forsake all for You. My life is all Yours. I want to obey You always"?

In your conversations with other believers, have you ever made claims like these? "I would never set my affection on the things of this world, even if I got a good-paying job"; "I would love my enemy if I had one"; "I would allow my husband or wife or children to go do Gospel work if God called them"; or "I would be faithful to Christ, even if my family disagrees with me and turns against me."

Did you know that every time you say "Amen" to a truth, everything you ever accepted by faith, anything you confessed, claimed or promised and all the teaching you agreed to in your heart—all this will be tested?

How do I know it will be tested? Throughout the Bible, God lets us know unmistakably that He is testing us, searching, trying, judging and examining our hearts and lives:

> "I, the LORD, search the heart, I test the mind" (Jeremiah 17:10).

> "But, O LORD of hosts, who judges righteously, who tries the feelings and the heart . . ." (Jeremiah 11:20).

> "For Thou hast tried us, O God; Thou hast refined us as silver is refined" (Psalm 66:10).

> "I am He who searches the minds and hearts" (Revelation 2:23).

In the parable of the seeds in Matthew 13, Jesus explains very clearly that every plant was tested by heat, birds and thorns after it had come up. When the sower sowed the seed, each ground received it; and each ground also was tested, along with the plants that grew out of it.

I am very much aware that the things I am writing to you in this book will not be forgotten by God. Everything I proclaim to you that has not yet been tested in my life, will be. I can wait for it.

But why would God want to test anyone if He is all-knowing, as the Bible says in these and many other Scriptures:

> "For the LORD searches all hearts, and understands every intent of the thoughts" (1 Chronicles 28:9).

> "For He knows the secrets of the heart" (Psalm 44:21).

> ". . . and able to judge the thoughts and intentions of the heart. . . . All things are open and laid bare to the eyes of Him" (Hebrews 4:12–13).

> "He did not need any one to bear witness concerning man for He Himself knew what was in man" (John 2:25).

According to these verses, God doesn't need to see the results from my testing. He knows me perfectly without it.

So why then would He want to test me? Because He wants *me* to see the truth about my life as well! The test is not at all for Him. The test is for *me*, because I don't know my own heart!

How many times do I look at myself and, even if I don't necessarily say it, think, "I am spiritual . . . I learned this . . . I am able to face that . . . I can bear that burden . . . I can withstand this temptation . . . I can teach others . . ."

But only God's test, not my thoughts or words, are "written" proof that I am who I claim to be.

Peter said in John 13:37, "I will lay down my life for You." I believe he was absolutely serious. He was convinced that his commitment and strength were sufficient to back up such a statement. Jesus knew better. When the test came, Peter probably was shocked and surprised at how little he actually knew himself.

Do you remember when you received the results of your school exams? The results proved three things: what you really knew, what you knew only a little, and what you did not know at all.

Every time God sows the seed of His Word into my life, He expects the seed to become plants with roots. Any such plants whose roots are not deep enough will not stand the test, whether it is a storm or intense heat.

Whatever is just "spiritual theory" and not practical in my life does not have deep enough roots, and *it is not* part of me. After the storm, the test results show me three things: what is real in my Christian life, what are areas I need to work on, and where God has to sow all over again.

EVERYONE WILL BE TESTED

Not only will everything be tested, but *everyone* who ever wanted to live and follow the Lord will be tested as well.

How do we know God doesn't make exceptions? We know because every person in the Bible, beginning with Adam and Eve and including even Jesus, was tested in some area of their lives.

Because human nature is a fallen nature, we are continually tempted and vulnerable to Satan's attacks. An unsaved person will continually fall prey to these attacks.

As believers, we have the Spirit of God living in us. He is able to give us victory over every attack. However, the presence of the Spirit of God does *not* eliminate attacks from the devil. Neither does it exempt us from being tested.

In fact, being a child of God *qualifies* us for testing. This may sound very negative and discouraging. But as we will discuss later, it is actually very positive and loving. Once we have become a child of God, God's interest in our development is undivided. In addition to disciplining us, caring for us and loving us, He also tests us. This is part of His plan to bring us to maturity.

In James 1:13, we read, "He Himself does not tempt any one." He only tests us. What is the difference?

Temptations are traps and attacks made with a single goal: to cause us to fall and to make a dead or badly wounded soldier out of us. The devil is the originator of temptations. He has no plans to let us get up again after we fall. His plan is to keep us flat on our face forever, unable to be used for God.

Tests are opportunities to evaluate our faith, our commitment and our obedience. They are checkpoints to make sure there is not a standstill in our growth or an abnormal development. Tests are given to help us determine where we are—*never* to make us fall. God is the One who tests us. He often uses circumstances, and He can even turn Satan's evil attacks or temptations into helpful tests. In these cases He gives us strength, clear guidance and His presence to overcome.

God watches carefully that the test is not above our spiritual ability to pass it. He doesn't give us a 10th-grade test when we are only studying 3rd-grade lessons. But He also expects us not to ask for an easy 4th-grade test when we are way above that level.

The goal of testing is this: to become stronger with every test passed.

Let us look at the lives of some Bible characters to see the tests they were asked to pass. Your circumstances may be different, but these will give you an idea of what kinds of tests might come your way also. I suggest you take your Bible and read these Scriptures.

Adam and Eve — Test of obedience to trust God's love and wisdom for their lives and souls (Genesis 2:17). Adam and Eve had never seen or experienced a world that was ruled by sin, death and destruction. Their lives were fulfilled and complete in every way. Therefore, they had nothing to compare with in order to understand the implications of Satan's offer. Yet they were called upon to trust God to know what was good for them.

Noah — Test of obedience to God's spoken word (Genesis 6:9, 14). Noah was the only one in his generation who was righteous and who walked with God. He was asked to do something that looked terribly foolish: to build an ark and to prepare for a flood, when it had never rained even once before on earth. Noah had many chances to change his mind during the next 120 years.

Abraham — Test of his love for the Lord (Genesis 22:2). Abraham had already passed the test of obedience when he left his country. Now he was tested *on the highest level:* to see if he loved God more than anything else, including his only son.

Job – Test of losing all yet not losing his faith (the book of Job). Job had lost everything, even his health. It looked as though God had forgotten him, had treated him unjustly or worse, was out to destroy him for no obvious reason. He had no knowledge about the conversation between God and Satan. Even though he could not understand why all these tragedies happened, he refused to give up his faith in his God. He declared: "Though He slay me, I will hope in Him" (Job 13:15) and "as for me, I know that my Redeemer lives" (Job 19:25).

Joseph – Test of purity (Genesis 39:6–20). Joseph was young when he was sold into Egypt. No one there cared if he kept the laws of Jehovah God or not. Yet Joseph had made up his mind not to sin against His God. Therefore, when he had opportunity to sin with Potiphar's wife, he ran from it, even though it cost him years of his life in prison.

Joseph – Test of his forgiveness (Genesis 45:1–11). When Joseph became the ruler of Egypt, he now had power, position and a chance to get even with his brothers. But he chose instead to forgive them, because he deliberately looked at the purpose of God in his life and not at the hurt his brothers had inflicted upon him.

Moses – Test of believing God to change the laws of nature (Exodus 14:16). Moses had to stretch out his rod to part the Red Sea. He had to try something *that was new.* No one had ever before believed God for such a thing.

Israel – Test of not one individual, but of the whole congregation together (Exodus 15:25, 16:4; Deuteronomy 8:2). As a people, the nation of Israel had seen God's mighty power, deliverance, miracles and provision. Now, based on all they knew about their God, He tested them to see if they would trust Him and follow His instructions as a whole body.

Joshua – Test of not trusting in his own strength or in strategic and military expertise (Joshua 6:3). By marching around Jericho, Joshua believed that God's plan would work better than his, even though God's plan looked more impossible and foolish than anything Joshua and his army would ever do on their own.

David – Test of believing in victory even if all the odds were against him, knowing by faith that God would deliver him (1 Samuel 17:32-52). With the decision, David put his life on the line, believing the battle was the Lord's and that He would give him the victory against Goliath, no matter how young, inexperienced and unqualified he was.

Prophets – Test of obedience to deliver God's message. Every time a prophet got a message, it was truly a test of his obedience to proclaim it. Most of the time, they had to bring messages that the people didn't like. Some of the prophets put their lives on the line to speak out against sin and proclaim destruction.

Daniel – Test of keeping God's commandment in a situation where everyone else had enough reason to compromise (Daniel 1:8, 6:10). As a young man, Daniel decided to keep the dietary laws God had commanded for Israel. He chose to go directly against the king's order and risk his own life rather than to compromise his faith like everyone else did. Later in his life, holding a high government office, he still put God's command above the king's. As a result, he ended up in the lion's den, but Daniel was willing to die there rather than join the others in disobeying God in order to save his life.

Jesus — Test of doing the will of the Father rather than His own (Luke 4:1–12, 22:42). During His temptation as well as in Gethsemane, Jesus had the chance to back out of going to the cross and make His mission on earth easier and more acceptable, with less suffering for Himself. But both times He rejected His own will and chose to do His Father's instead. If He would have chosen His own, we still would be lost without a Savior.

How Is the Testing Done?

In the parable of the seed (Matthew 13:3–9, 18–23), Jesus not only spoke of the different types of testing each plant faced, but He also gave an explanation of what it would mean in our lives.

When we read about the birds, thorns, heat, rocky ground and good ground, we realize that the test here is a combination of external enemies and circumstances, and internal heart problems.

The outside enemies and circumstances are represented by the birds that snatch the seed, the thorns that choke the plants and the intense heat that dries them up. These are the fear of persecution, cares of this world and the deceitfulness of riches. External attacks are designed to sidetrack our attention from the Word of God that has been sown in our hearts and to eventually remove it altogether.

The *inside problems* are represented by the lack of

prepared ground, both the wayside and the rocky ground. These are hard and unprepared hearts that give the enemy the opportunity to win the battle.

Jesus also told the parable of the house built on the sand and the house built on the rock (Matthew 7:24–27). When we examine the test that came upon both houses, we again find a mixture of outside enemies and inside problems.

The *outside enemies* are the rain, flood and storm, which can be seen as persecution, tragedies and severe circumstances that are not caused by us.

The *inside problem* is again the ground: sand. The heart makes a foolish choice to build on religion, church membership or any other foundation than Jesus alone.

This is *not* just a parable to show who is a true believer and who is not. This parable is very, very relevant in the lives of believers. We chose the right foundation—Jesus—when we got saved. But since then, we may have poured a lot of sand on our good foundation, trying to build our Christian life on a special revelation, important denominational traditions, respect we demand from others, a position we hold in the church or a spiritual gift we received from the Lord. All this and more will turn out to be only treacherous sand when the storm comes.

Peter tells us in 1 Peter 1:7 and 4:12 that we are "tested by fire," just as gold is. He even calls it a "fiery ordeal." To refine gold is truly a long ordeal and a hot one!

The Old Testament tells us about a test in King Hezekiah's life that was different than usual.

According to 2 Kings 18:5–6, there was no one who trusted the Lord so completely as Hezekiah. Yet 2 Chronicles 32:31 tells us that "God left him alone only to test him," meaning that God didn't tell him what to do in that particular situation.

According to Hezekiah's spiritual understanding, his previous experience and his knowledge about God and His Word, he should have made the right decision—but he failed. This shows that even the greatest men and women of God couldn't pass a single test if God were to take away His guidance even for a moment. This should keep us humble!

REASONS FOR FAILING A TEST

There are times when we fail a test and we just can't understand why. Let us look at five common reasons for failing a test:

One, we fail because we never did a self-evaluation.

Second Corinthians 13:5 says, "Test yourselves to see if you are in the faith; examine yourselves! . . . Unless indeed you fail the test?"

Our children attend a school where they have workbooks in each subject. After completing each book, they take a 3- to 4-page self-test. These pages are a summary of all the main things they studied in the workbook. This self-test shows them exactly whether or not they understand the subject and if they have learned enough to be able to pass the *real test* that will be given the following day! If they make too many mistakes on the self-test, they still have a whole day to go back and study the right answers. The self-test shows them what they really know, *before* it gets serious. Once they are able to pass their self-test with good results, they have the best chance to pass well in the real test also.

This is exactly what Paul tried to teach the Corinthians and us. We must stop and evaluate our walk. Practically, this means we must ask ourselves questions like these:

"The gift I gave to my brother—was it really out of concern for him, or did I want to impress him and the church with my generosity?"

"The way I talked to my husband this morning— was it really loving and truthful, or did I try to hide my bitter attitude behind a smile?"

"The prayer or testimony I said at church—was it my desire to lift up Jesus, or was it my secret wish that everyone would know how well I did this week?"

Two, we fail because when the pressure comes, we act like Peter on the water instead of Jesus (Matthew 14:30).

Like Peter, we start out well. We trust the Lord to see us through the problem we face. But all of a sudden, we look at the problem and realize that our strength is not enough and that all of the solutions we can come up with are not sufficient to conquer this mountain.

We start to try whatever we can think of, and we fail. We sink!

What we forgot when we took our eyes off Jesus was that God has solutions in store that we can't even imagine! We stopped trusting the Lord because in our heart we put

Him down on our level. We didn't voice it out, but our actions really said, "God, I wanted to trust You, but in the middle of the storm I realized the size of the problem. You will surely not be able to find any better solution than the three I already thought of. So, I will try mine and see if they work."

The trouble with this "logical" approach is that God has the power to do something "illogical," something impossible. He has the power to create and to call something into being from nothing.

Therefore, it *always* pays off to trust Him until the end and not lose our trust in the middle of the event.

Three, we fail because we rely on our own wisdom.

In 1 Samuel 13:8, we read how Saul waited and waited for Samuel the prophet to come and offer the sacrifice. Finally, he decided that he was running out of time, and he had to take things into his own hands. He justified his action by the pressure of time and circumstances. God was just too slow; therefore, he had to use his common sense to get things going. He thought God would understand the compromise, because this was a genuine emergency!

Yet God didn't accept his reasoning. He had tested Saul to see if he would go ahead without God's way of guidance—and Saul failed the test.

How about in our lives? We pray for an answer, we pray for guidance, we wait; but no answer seems to come our way. We pray some more and we wait for a few days longer. Then all of a sudden, we decide:

"This is it! If God doesn't give us the answer by Saturday, we will go ahead and start on the project! There is no point in waiting around any longer. We are not only losing precious time, but we are missing out on the best opportunities. If we don't act now, our competition will get all the profit. God surely doesn't want us to be foolish and miss out on a good thing like this. Maybe His answer is for us to get going and He will confirm it later."

We are right! God doesn't want us to miss out on a good thing, but we *always* will if we go ahead without His guidance. After all, only He knows if the "good thing" we are going after is a loser in the end or not!

What we actually have done is given God an ultimatum: "Lord, You have until Saturday to answer us. If You don't, You will just have to accept our plans and bless them. Amen!"

You know, this is the surest way to fail in your own life, your family life, your business and especially in your ministry!

As in Saul's case, God may have already planned long ago to tell us His answer not on Saturday, but on Sunday. In 1 Samuel 13:10, Samuel came as soon as Saul finished the burnt offering.

The end of Saul's story was that his kingdom was taken from him.

Relying on our own wisdom reveals the pride of our heart. We actually make ourselves equal with God, thinking we are qualified to alter His plans and tell Him what needs to be done and when.

The worst place to rely on our own wisdom is in God's work itself. We can't build or lead God's kingdom with human reason and wisdom. It just doesn't work. Just like in Saul's case, everything will eventually crumble.

Four, we fail because during the test we do not seek the Lord's counsel.

A classic example is the story in Joshua 9:3–15. Joshua wanted to serve the Lord with all his heart. He was diligent to keep His commandments, and he had no intentions of acting apart from God's revealed laws.

But he overlooked one thing: The enemies he was dealing with were not playing fair. They didn't abide by the rules; they lied and played tricks. Joshua was such a righteous man that his words meant exactly what he had in his heart. He assumed that the men who talked with him were as honest as he was.

Joshua didn't want to rebel against the Lord or ignore the Lord's guidance. The facts just looked so clear and unmistakably obvious that he thought he knew the right answer and didn't need to bother God unnecessarily. Together with the elders, he thought that they could make a decision simply on the basis of the facts and find the right answer from the laws God had already laid down for them.

That would have worked out all right if the enemies hadn't hidden a trap in their contract. Even with Joshua being such an outstanding man of God and surely an experienced leader, he was not able to detect the lie. Only God, who is all-knowing, would have revealed the lie *simply by asking* for His counsel!

In our lives, we come across situations that look so clear and so obvious that we make decisions on the basis of the matching answer from the Bible. This is right and we must do so! But we also must remember: Our enemy does not always give us all the facts! Whenever he can, he makes a trap or slips a lie into something that looks so clear and innocent. We may have the right answer from God's Word for the obvious facts, but we can't take into consideration the hidden facts. So our answer is incomplete, maybe even wrong.

God wants us to learn to rely on His counsel, even if we think we know the right answer. We are only safe in our decisions if we include God's counsel in all of them, even the easy ones!

Five, we fail because we have never settled the question of whom we will serve.

There was a time when I thought it was normal for someone who gave his life to Christ to follow Jesus alone and serve Him only.

But over the years, I have learned that many of my brothers and sisters have a difficult time making decisions, even in their everyday lives.

One day a girl came to visit me. She told me about the difficult time she had going with her parents to a church that clearly didn't preach the Gospel. She had given her life to Christ two years before while she worked in another town. Now she had moved back home, and she didn't want to disappoint her parents who weren't saved. She said she was unhappy and didn't know what she should do.

Another girl wrote me a letter, asking me to please pray for the man she wanted to marry, that he would be saved. She didn't want to marry an unbeliever, but at the same time she was not willing to give up this man.

Others I have met were struggling with whether or not they as a Christian could go to certain places or if it was all right to say a half truth, to take just a little bribe, to cheat a little bit on a test or to go to a church that didn't preach salvation by faith.

I admit not all decisions are easy to make, and many times I, too, have a hard time.

But there is one thing that will eliminate most of these struggles and will simplify the rest! I call it the most important decision next to salvation—*it is the decision of whom I will serve!* Once I have made up my mind and have clarified my position, every other decision will fall into place.

Then when my parents ask me to compromise my faith, when my friends at school want me to join them in violating the school rules, when I have the opportunity to make a profit just by telling a lie—then there is no longer any debate in my mind. I have decided to follow Jesus and serve Him alone. My decision is settled for good. I will not compromise, even if I have to stand alone! There is no turning back.

We fail so much because with every new situation, we try to figure out *afresh* what standpoint we should take this time. By then, we are in the middle of a test and are so emotionally involved that we often lack the clarity and sober ability to choose what is right.

The strength of Joshua's life and leadership is expressed in Joshua 24:15: "But as for me and my house, we will serve the LORD."

When we look at Joshua's success as a leader, we can easily recognize that he made this decision not at the end of his life, but as a young man. When he was sent to spy out the land of Canaan, he and Caleb were the only ones who determined to trust and obey the Lord in spite of the impossible task ahead and in spite of their whole nation's rebellion and disobedience.

God expects us to become immovable in our faith. Yet this is impossible unless we make up our minds once and for all eternity whom we will serve and, from then on, follow through with it.

WHAT HAPPENS AFTER WE HAVE FAILED A TEST?

Looking at the Bible, we are in some ways surprised to see how many of the heroes of faith recorded in Hebrews 11 failed tests during their lifetimes. We discover the same fact in the lives of the Old Testament prophets, the New Testament apostles and the early Christians.

Yet God talks about them as examples for our lives, as men and women of God of whom the world is not worthy. Let us look at just a few incidents when these examples didn't pass the test:

- *Abraham failed* – When he lied and said his wife was his sister. He also failed when he had his son Ishmael, trying to assist God in providing the promised son.

- *Moses failed* – When he hit the rock instead of speaking to it.

- *David failed* – When he took a census of Israel instead of trusting God. He also failed when he committed adultery and murder and then tried to hide it.

- *Elijah failed* – When he was afraid of Jezebel and ran away, wanting to die instead of trusting God to protect him.

- *Jonah failed* – When he ran away and didn't want to go to Nineveh.

- *Peter failed* – When he denied the Lord and also later when he tried to compromise his conviction about the equality of believers from different backgrounds.

- *The disciples failed* – When they deserted Jesus.

- *Paul failed* – When he quarreled with Barnabas.

God could have easily prevented these failures from being recorded in the Bible. That way we could have had real heroes who were perfect. But God deliberately wanted these examples to be remembered along with their failures.

Why? For our sakes. This way, we can identify with them, realizing that they were no different than we are. At the same time, they are a model for us, showing God's forgiveness, God's grace and God's ability to pick up those who have fallen and failed and restore them completely. Not only does God restore them, but He also makes their lives examples and blessings for generations to come.

Looking at these examples and at the Word of God, we know without a doubt that God will not throw us away after we have failed. He still loves us, and He still wants to use us! He expects us to repent and to walk with Him again.

His compassion for us after we fail is so much greater than we can ever imagine.

But like a good teacher, God doesn't just skip the test we failed. He will explain our failure to us, and He has a way to make us study the *same* lesson over again. He prepares us for another test on same subject! He will not go on with our education until we pass this test. The reason for this is that these tests are foundation stones, which will carry the weight of the rest of the building to come. If one of these foundation stones crumbles later, the whole building might fall.

Let us therefore not be stubborn, but rather be willing to repeat a lesson so that our usefulness for the Lord will not be hindered.

God's Ultimate Goals for Testing

As I mentioned previously, the goal of testing is to make us stronger with every test passed. This is very true, but God has far higher plans than that:

- James 1:4 reveals God's purpose fully: "that you may be perfect and complete, lacking in nothing."

- First Peter 1:7 shows the quality of Christian we ought to become through testing: "more precious than gold." This phrase leaves no doubt that we are to become absolutely real, genuine, and pure having no less than permanent value!

- Matthew 13:8 tells us that our roots will become

deep, we will be immovable and we will produce multiplied abundant fruit for the kingdom of God.

• Ephesians 4:13 expresses God's desire for us to grow up "to a mature man, to the measure of the stature which belongs to the fulness of Christ." This passage by itself doesn't talk about testing, but that our maturity depends on teaching and learning. From studying all our other Scriptures, however, we have seen that there is no deep learning unless it is continually accompanied by testing.

Results after We Have Passed the Test

The truth we once only accepted and knew in theory has become part of our very lives!

We have become more mature, more useful and better equipped to serve our Lord.

Not only have we come a step closer to God's goals for our lives, but passing the test has brought "praise and glory and honor" to Jesus (1 Peter 1:7).

If God Would Never Test Us on Earth

Have you ever imagined what would happen if God listened to our complaints and groanings and granted us our wish to always live happily after our salvation and never to face one test? This is what would happen:

We would, of course, do a lot of good works for Him and add much spiritual knowledge to our lives. We would look forward to seeing Him face-to-face.

Then, finally, one day we would die; with great excitement and joy we would walk through the pearly gate to meet our Savior, whom we have longed to see for so many years.

Along with us, we have brought a "truckload" of prizes and trophies we intend to present to Jesus our Lord and to lay at His feet. What a day, what a thrill!

Then Jesus will look at all the great trophies we brought with us, and lovingly He will say, "I am so glad you worked so hard for me, but before you can lay the prizes at my feet, they need to be approved . . . by fire."

Before we can ask any further questions, the attending angel takes all our prizes and puts them, one after another, in a fire that burns nearby.

Because we are sure that all our trophies are made out of pure gold and silver and some even out of precious stones, we have no objections, because we know heat will not damage them.

But as we watch the trophies being placed in the fire, to our horror, we see them go up in smoke, one after another. All that is left behind is a small pile of ashes. Our first thought is that something is wrong with our eyesight, or perhaps there is a mix-up of trophies or something wrong with the fire. But after checking and ruling out all these possibilities, for the first time in our Christian life we go and pick up one of the remaining trophies to check it out. We scratch the gold a little with our fingernail, and to our surprise, it peels off easily and uncovers the wood underneath.

We are speechless, terrified and despairing as the test of fire continues until the last of our trophies is consumed;

with it, our last hope to lay something at the feet of Jesus — the One who had died for us — is destroyed.

We have reached heaven; we are saved. We have seen our Savior face-to-face, and we will live with Him for all eternity. But when He calls out our name at the Judgment Seat, we have to stand before Him empty-handed, with nothing to lay at His feet. He wanted to give us a reward, maybe even a crown, but we have brought nothing for which He can give it. Forever we have missed the joy of this moment — because we never tested ourselves and didn't allow God to test us and our fruits while living on earth.

Dear believer, once we are in the presence of God, all is over. It is too late to correct anything.

Jesus loves us more than we can ever imagine. His desire for us is that the day when our works pass through the test of fire will be a day full of excitement and great joy. He wants so much to be able to give us a reward. He longs to tell us that we did well, that we were faithful and that our fruit remained. He doesn't want to see us disappointed.

Because He knows how happy it will make us to bring something to Him, He tests us and our works here on earth. In this way He gives us the opportunity to correct, to change and to rebuild — until our work and life are truly gold, silver and precious stones that will pass the test of fire.

Do you understand and see that His testing is born out of love for you? The more you recognize the depth of His love, the more you will also yield to His testing.

7. THE COST IS TOO HIGH

There I was, on my way to the repair store to pick up my sewing machine. Only five minutes before, I had talked to the owner of the shop on the phone. As soon as I hung up the receiver, I knew exactly what was going to happen: The Lord would not let me have any peace unless I went and asked this man to forgive me for becoming angry with him on the phone.

I KNOW HE WILL NOT LET ME GET AWAY WITH IT

A small part on my sewing machine had broken two weeks before, and I took it to be fixed. At the shop I was told that it would be checked and repaired right away, but two weeks had gone by, and the job wasn't done. Several times I had called, and every time I was promised that it would be ready soon.

Now I was running out of time. In two days my

husband had to leave for the mission field, and I desperately needed the machine to repair his clothes.

I had definitely been treated wrong, and there, in the middle of my phone call, I ran out of patience! With an angry voice I told the owner what I thought of his kind of business dealings. The shop owner reacted to my words by getting even angrier than I was. He said all kinds of things back to me. In the end I told him that I was going to pick up my machine right then and take it somewhere else.

Looking back at this conversation, I almost couldn't believe that I had done this. I was a Christian, and I felt ashamed before the Lord at how I had completely failed to be any kind of testimony. I asked the Lord to forgive me, and I told Him that I would go and make it right, because *I knew* He wouldn't leave me alone about this until I did it.

Because my children were with me, I explained to them what I had done and that I needed to go and ask this man for forgiveness. When we arrived at the shop, I told Daniel and Sarah to wait outside. The man had already sounded so angry on the phone that I was afraid he would "blow up" altogether when he saw me. Therefore, I decided that it was better if the children were at a safe distance.

With a prayer, I entered the store. Before the man could say anything, I told him that I was wrong to get angry with him on the phone and that I was sorry for doing it.

Remembering the phone call, I expected "thunder and lightning." But to my surprise, he told me that he too was sorry about his words and reactions and the neglect of his shop. He offered to repair my machine within one day — and he did!

When I left the store, I felt so glad about how the Lord

had straightened out what I had messed up. The children, of course, wanted to know every detail, and I had the opportunity to teach them about confessing and asking forgiveness when we do wrong.

MOTIVES FOR OBEDIENCE

Believers have different motives for their obedience to the Lord.

Some are afraid of possible punishment, such as sickness, accidents or even death. Others are very concerned about the crowns, rewards and mansions they would miss out on when they go to heaven.

I hardly ever think about possible rewards or punishments. Looking at my life, I see just two basic motives for my obedience to Jesus:

- I obey out of love.

- I obey because the cost of repentance is too high!

God uses both of these motives to keep me on track. Yet the first one, obedience out of love, is definitely the better one and surely His first choice for my walk with Him.

OBEDIENCE OUT OF LOVE

This should be our normal response to anything the Lord asks us to do or not to do. He has given us a new heart and a new Spirit, and we are new creatures. Our new heart is created in such a way that we are sensitive and responsive to His love rather than to the threat of the law. Our new desire is to respond back to the Lord with obedience out of love rather than by force.

But I have noticed that I am not always at the same spiritual level every hour or every day of my life. There are times when I am more tired, weaker because I am facing trials and difficulties; maybe I am overworked, or my heart has a touch of rebellion. Some of these things have occasionally affected my obedience out of love. It shouldn't have happened, but it did.

OBEDIENCE OUT OF FEAR OF THE COST OF REPENTANCE

There are a lot of Scriptures in the Bible that talk about the fear of the Lord and that we must have it. One even says, "The fear of the LORD is the beginning of wisdom" (Proverbs 9:10).

Some of the Scriptures talk about the reverence we should show to God. Others talk about the punishment that will follow if we do not respect His commandments and do not fear Him enough to do His will.

I have learned that if I can't find enough love in my heart to obey Him, then I at least must find enough fear to do His will—otherwise I will get in trouble.

In order to help me obey, Jesus has often had to resort to serious measures. He reminds me how bitter and hard it has been to go back and confess, repent and make things right later. When He talks to me in that way, He never forgets to remind me that He has never let me get away with anything so far, and He is not going to do it this time either!

Many times this "threat" of the cost of repentance does

work "miracles" of obedience. I doubt that this kind of motive will bring any great rewards in heaven, but I am thankful that at least it keeps me from wrong. Sometimes I am amazed at the kind of avenues the Lord, in His love, chooses to use to help us obey Him anyway, even if *our* love for Him fails!

THE COST OF REPENTANCE IS VERY HIGH

In the beginning of this chapter, I told you the story of my sewing machine. It was hard to go back and straighten things out, but the visible consequences were not much more than being humbled, embarrassed and ashamed. However, I remember several occasions in my life when I compromised my obedience, and my subsequent confession could have brought very difficult consequences. I will share one of them with you.

I was 16 and I had been a Christian for about two years when the time came to take my final school exam. It was hard, but I had predetermined to be absolutely honest in all the tests. Just before we had to write our English, spelling and dictation test, however, someone came to tell our class the answers. Through some kind of mix-up, he had obtained 8 or 10 of these difficult spelling words. Everyone tried to hear and memorize this important information, including me.

During the exam, all of us used this knowledge to make good marks. In fact, it turned out that our class was the only one out of four classes to get these answers right. Our test results were so obviously good and "exclusive" that the teachers became suspicious. Our teacher came and asked us where we got the information. He called out many of the students by name to give him a personal explanation. Each of them told a different lie. I was glad he didn't call on me. The truth never came out.

After graduation, everyone went for further studies. I went to a boarding school to learn home economics, which was a prerequisite to enter nursing school. I was too young to go to nursing school yet, but I applied anyway and was told that I would be accepted after I completed my home economic studies. My primary goal was not to lose any time in preparing myself for the mission field.

In the meantime, the Lord had not forgotten my compromise. He began talking to my heart, showing me that I had joined my classmates in doing wrong by choosing to listen to the answers and by keeping quiet when the teacher asked for the truth. I had cheated by not walking away, and I had lied by keeping quiet!

Furthermore, the Lord told me that I needed to confess. Two years before this, He had called me to serve Him, and now He made it clear to me that I couldn't, unless my walk with Him was totally clear. He gave me a very hard requirement, and I knew exactly what it might cost me if I obeyed:

- I could lose my diploma.

- Without this diploma, I couldn't be accepted in nursing school or in the Bible school I wanted to attend.

- No mission board would take me without my diploma either.

- The school might ask me to come back and repeat a whole year and write all the exams again. I would lose a whole year of my life.

- In addition to all this, what embarrassment I would cause for my family and myself. I was sure that everybody would think I was absolutely foolish and that it was totally unnecessary to tell anyone about such a small thing. After all, it was only a matter of maybe 8 or 10 words!

- How angry my fellow students would be if I revealed their secrets also.

During the following days, the Lord taught me that nothing else in this world was as important as following Him and obeying Him. I must deny myself and love Him more than my diploma, my future plans and my parents, even if I were to lose them all.

I remember so well the day when I made the decision that I would love the Lord first and do what He had asked me to do. I wrote a letter to my teacher, explaining to him that I had not been honest in my English exam. The letter was only about myself—I didn't accuse or reveal anything about my classmates.

My heart was trembling when I mailed this letter—I knew that with it, I was laying down even the very call that God had put on my life. As I obeyed the Lord, my heart was filled with such joy and peace, knowing that it was better to please Him than to compromise my walk with Him.

It had been a very hard test of my love for the Lord. At

the same time it was my first unforgettable lesson about *the cost of repentance.* I had found out that it was definitely very high, and it is better to obey in the first place than have to repent later on.

The Lord was so good to me, and the school didn't do anything to my diploma.

Knowing the cost of repentance is an extra protection for our walk. Once you have tasted the cost of repentance, you really don't want to pay it a second time. Occasionally when my friends try to point out how "spiritually" I behaved in certain situations, I tell them, "I did this, not because I am so spiritual, but because the cost of repentance is too high!"

The Cost of Not Repenting

In your own life, you may have already decided that the cost of repentance is too high or the matter you need to confess too difficult or insignificant. I would like for you to now look for a moment at the cost of *not* repenting:

- You must realize that when God convicts your heart and you don't obey, you are actively resisting the Holy Spirit.

- If you don't give in soon, you will automatically try to shut this voice out of your heart, because it is impossible to bear such a constant reminder for such a long time.

- This will result in a loss of sensitivity to God's voice.

- A crack will begin to show in your love relationship with the Lord, because obedience is the proof of your love for Him.

- Your joy and peace will suffer.

- Your longing to spend time in prayer and fellowship with the Lord will vanish, because you know that each time you come into His presence, He will remind you of this deficit in your obedience.

- The end result is that your effectiveness, your strength, your spiritual power and your whole Christian life are greatly weakened.

By looking at these results, we can easily conclude that yes, the cost of repentance is very high, but the cost of *not* repenting is even higher!

A HALF-REPENTANCE IS NOT ENOUGH

Once you have failed in your obedience to the Lord, there is nothing else you can do to restore your pure walk with the Lord other than to repent. Most of us do ask the Lord for His forgiveness. This is right if we have sinned only against Him.

But if it involves others, it is not enough just to ask pardon from the Lord!

Many Christians are totally unwilling to go all the way, to confess and ask forgiveness from others. Why? It could be that it's too embarrassing, they fear they will lose their respect, or they may get in trouble because of the consequences that such a confession might bring about.

All this is not their deepest problem. The root problem for not being willing to confess is pride and rebellion.

WAS IT ALL FOR NOTHING?

There were a few occasions in my life when I too struggled with how I could avoid the cost of repentance after I had failed. The only answer I could come up with was that I would have to compromise my commitment to the Lord.

I remember well how the Lord seemed to be right there in my room, and He asked me these questions:

> "I have walked with you for so many years—do you want to turn back now?"

> "Remember the price you paid to follow Me. Will you make it all void?"

> "You have come through so many battles and difficulties—were they all for nothing?"

These questions from Him would bring tears to my eyes, and they helped me choose to follow Him those times as well.

8. REALITY

When Jesus walked on this earth, people soon began to realize clearly that there was something about Him that set Him apart from everyone else. It was not His looks, His clothes or His speech — it was His life of reality.

You see, He had come into a world where it is normal to cover up facts, hide failures and pretend success, a world where people go to great lengths to make it to the top and where money, connections and advertising buy a lot of fame and glory.

When people met Jesus, they had to admit: He was real through and through! There was nothing false in anything He did, taught or proclaimed about Himself. His personal life was without reproach and corresponded completely with His convictions and His teaching. The miracles were genuine; there were no tricks involved and no staged healings. His prayers were incredible, and everybody could see that His Father answered all of them, in detail! His love was so overwhelming, lasting and so different from anything people had ever encountered before. He even managed to forgive and love those who betrayed Him and nailed Him to the cross. Truly His ability to love was out of this world! Like other preachers, Jesus made a number of prophecies; but to the people's amazement, His were accurate and came to pass exactly as He had said.

All in all, there was absolutely nothing in His life that contradicted God's Word or anything He Himself claimed. He literally lived what He preached. He had many enemies who wished Him dead a thousand times. They tried to trap Him, stone Him and have Him killed in any way possible. They accused Him of a lot of things, but none of them could stand up and accuse Him of hypocrisy.

JESUS REVEALED THE FATHER

Jesus lived an absolutely transparent life, with no fenced yard, walls or locked doors. He wanted people to watch Him and observe Him! Why? Because He had come to show them, by His life and nature, what God the Father was like and how the Father would feel, talk, act, teach and love them. In other words, with His very life, He painted a picture before their eyes, including in it every detail of His and their heavenly Father.

So far, no one had seen the Father. All that they had heard and read about Him was wrapped into a cloud of mystery, terror, judgment, thunder and lightning. True, there was more revelation than that in the Old Testament, but for His people, there was always quite a distant, fearful approach to meet their God.

With Jesus walking among them, for the first time God could be touched, observed, loved and asked personal questions. They could receive individual counsel and be healed, comforted and encouraged. For the first time, they could come very close to Him.

When people looked at Him, they saw exactly what Hebrews 1:3 describes: "He is the radiance of His [the Father's] glory and the exact representation of His nature." Jesus simply told them, "He who has seen Me has seen the Father" (John 14:9).

His whole life was wrapped up and consumed with this one goal: to be such a true and clear representation of God the Father that even the most sinful man on earth could recognize God's love for him and desire to be born again.

WE ARE TO REVEAL CHRIST

Jesus didn't stop His mission here. He told His disciples: "As the Father has sent Me, I also send you" (John 20:21). This call was not just to work for Him, but that they too should portray the Father to the world, exactly as He was doing it.

After almost 2,000 years, this call still stands. He expects me to be the exact representation of Him in the same measure that He is the exact representation of the Father.

Paul expresses the same thought when he writes to the Corinthian church: ". . . in everything commending ourselves as servants of God" (2 Corinthians 6:4). They saw themselves as servants, just as Jesus had been their example of a servant. Now in *all* areas of their life and ministry, they were portraying Jesus' way and life of servanthood to the people around them.

Paul gave such an accurate picture of Jesus with his own life that he could tell the believers and their leaders: "Be imitators of me, just as I also am of Christ" (1 Corinthians 11:1).

Portraying Jesus with my life is not a joke or just a part-time job! It is a lifetime calling and an awesome responsibility. The people who hear me, see me and live around me *must* be able to see the reality of the nature of the living God! They must see the exact picture, not a distortion!

How Real Are We?

As we realize the seriousness of this call, we must look at ourselves and find out how real we are. We need to discover if our representation of God accurately represents the Lord or not.

As Christians, most of the time we evaluate things we do by their success or if others do them also. Instead, let us evaluate our Christian lives according to reality and with total honesty. We can't afford to do the wrong things if we represent Christ Himself.

In order to evaluate ourselves, we need to ask these six questions regarding every area of our life and walk:

1. Is it real or do I make it up with my emotions or knowledge?

2. Is it real or do I imitate others?

3. Does it represent God Himself — or me or my denomination?

4. Did God ask me to do it?

5. Do I have God's approval and witness?

6. Do my words and actions correspond, or is my life lying?

Let us look now at some areas of our Christian life:

- *Your salvation.* Is it holding you up or do you try to hold it up? In other words, do you have His witness in your heart that you are born again? Is there evidence—true spiritual fruit?

- *Your walk with Jesus.* Is it the same walk at home in your family and with your neighbors that you proclaim at church?

- *Your giving.* Is it unto the Lord, or is it to be seen?

- *Your smile and your kindness.* Is it just culture, or is it from the heart?

- *Your clapping, your raising hands in prayer, your "Hallelujah, Amen, Praise the Lord."* Is the reason for these based on tradition or true praise and worship?

- *Your close relationship with the Lord and your love for Him.* Are these real or only a facade before others?

- *Your prayers and singing.* Are they from your heart?

- *Your testimony.* Are you backing up your witnessing with your life?

- *Your humility.* Is it just a front or truly of your heart, resulting from knowing Jesus? Do you use it to impress others?

- *Your love for others.* Does it limited to only the people you enjoy being around? Does it cross over poverty and caste systems? Do you use so-called "love" for gain of money, position and so on?

- *The Holy Spirit in you.* Are you truly filled with God's Spirit, or do you imitate others? The evidence is a Spirit-controlled life!

- *Your spiritual gifts.* Do you seek to build up the Body of Christ? Do you use your gifts with great care and under the authority of those who are placed by God to lead the church? Do you have a life that backs up your gift? Are they all given by the Lord Himself? Do you want to impress others? Are you using these gifts with discipline according to the rules Paul wrote down in 1 Corinthians 14? In exercising your gifts, is your every word truly worthy of proclaiming, "Thus says the Lord . . ."? Do you know without *any* shadow of a doubt that your message is absolutely the Lord's and not just some thoughts of your own heart? It is a fearful thing to say, "Thus says the Lord" when in reality He never said anything! Do you use these gifts for your own gain, honor or fame?

There is so much more that we need to check out to discover if what we do is real! God hates lies. We might not say lies, but we might live them if we portray a spirituality that is not real.

Our life has to be approved by God Himself. Because we represent not ourselves but Him, He must be able to put His signature under each one of our actions and words. With this signature, He can testify to this world and to the Spirit world, "Yes, this is exactly like I am, the words I say, the places I go," and so on.

As we bear His name, let us live a life worthy of our calling!

9. Re-created Revival

I had the opportunity to visit a wax museum with hundreds of re-created, life-size historical figures.

There were famous presidents, world leaders, generals, pioneers, criminals, artists, singers, scientists, astronauts and sports champions. All of them were created out of wax and were perfected to the exact detail of color, hair and clothing. Many even had mechanical movements, allowing them to turn their head and look at you or perform a task with their hand. They were so real that you unconsciously took a step back when you first "met" them. Whole scenes out of history were re-created, such as a battle, a debate, an assassination, the signing of a treaty and so on. At a number of these scenes you could press a button and add the movements. The voices and sound effects made everything seem even more "real" and "alive."

I stayed longer at a few scenes to study every detail and to read the historical account. While I was there, a number of other visitors passed by, and all of them pressed the same buttons to create the movements and voices. After watching the general raise his arm and utter the same command 20 times, the scene lost a little of its reality.

Even though every detail was perfectly re-created, one thing was missing: the actual *life*. You see, true life is fresh, spontaneous, new, changing and creative.

ALMOST ALIVE

In many churches, fellowships and groups I have visited, I have felt as I did in that wax museum. But not always at the first visit, of course.

Often the first impression of the singing, the clapping, the testimonies, the worship, the altar call, the exercising of gifts and so on looked so real — like true revival or a true moving of the Holy Spirit. But slowly, after a few visits, I realized that much of it was created and re-created as with the pressing of a button. Shall I call it a "holy tradition" or "sight-and-sound effects" that must be there at any cost?

As in the museum, every detail of revival is perfectly re-created. The only thing missing is the real life!

WHY DO WE RE-CREATE OUR SPIRITUAL HISTORY?

As in the museum, we want to *preserve* an important moment, *relive* an experience, or *bring back* a lost glory! Let us look at some possible examples:

Two years ago, there were several genuine prophecies from the Lord in a church, which came to pass.

Now the believers want to preserve the reputation of their church as a prophesying church.

A brother had a special encounter with the Lord at a prayer meeting. God's presence and power were so real, and this event changed his entire life. Whenever this believer comes to church now, his greatest wish is to relive this experience again.

There was much persecution followed by a genuine revival in a village 20 years ago. Many Hindus were saved, and miracles happened. There was much rejoicing, excitement and fear of God among the believers. Those in the church who tasted it at that time want to bring it back.

How Do We Re-create?

One, we look at the past events and we notice the "symptoms" that accompanied those events. Consider these examples:

- *Loud weeping* – because of genuine repentance.

- *Shouting* – for joy, realizing God's forgiveness.

- *Embracing each other* – as God's love flooded our whole being, and we truly loved our fellow believers.

- *Raising our hands* – in true surrender and worship.

95

- *Kneeling or prostrating* – realizing the majesty of the King of kings.

- *Dancing and jumping* – at the sight of a miracle.

- *Singing, clapping and beating the drum for hours* – we couldn't contain the praise that filled our hearts.

- *Spontaneous prayer meetings at 5 A.M. at church* – we longed to be in His presence so much. It was the greatest joy to be there.

Two, the events are past, but we continue to display the symptoms as if the events are happening right now. The remembrance is still fresh, and people are happy to praise God in very expressive terms.

Three, years have gone by. New converts have joined the church. They never saw the revival we had years ago. Neither did they go through any suffering, as the old believers once faced. Yet we teach them the symptoms of a revival they never experienced. We teach them to shout, dance, beat the drums for hours and so on. We teach them not only to act out these things every time they come, but also that without these symptoms, their Christian and church lives are missing the key elements.

We Are Asked to Remember, Not to Re-create

Many Bible verses tell us over and over to remember past experiences with God, words said by Jesus, examples given by the Old Testament saints and so on. Yet nowhere in the whole Bible do we read that we should re-create an event.

Remembrance of God's power, faithfulness, protection and love always strengthens our faith. As we reflect back, it prepares us to trust the Lord for the battles ahead of us.

Re-creation always weakens our faith, because it is not backed up by reality. We can only pretend so long until our spiritual sensitivity becomes dull. In addition, re-creation actually makes us hypocrites. We pretend to have a spiritual experience this very moment that is in reality not there.

DISCERNMENT

God wants us to be able to discern real from false in every area of our Christian lives.

In a revival atmosphere, worship expressions or the exercising of spiritual gifts, it is often difficult to make a distinction between spiritual and fleshly motivation. Much of it is mixed: Remembrance, reality and re-creation are often cooked together in one stew.

How can we know the difference?

The Holy Spirit comes or falls upon people. Every biblical account of believers being filled or empowered, both the first time and subsequent times, is described by words like:

"The Holy Spirit *fell upon* all those who were listening" (Acts 10:44).

"The gift of the Holy Spirit had been *poured out*"
(Acts 10:45).

"The Holy Spirit *fell upon* them" (Acts 11:15).

"They *were all filled* with the Holy Spirit" (Acts 2:4).

"And when they had prayed, the place where they
had gathered together *was shaken,* and they *were all
filled* with the Holy Spirit" (Acts 4:31).

Nowhere in the Bible do we read that the believers were
shaking the place or producing a noise like a rushing wind
in order to bring about the filling of the Holy Spirit.

Neither is there any account that they were filled with
power by forcing it to happen through repetitions of jumping, dancing, screaming, beating instruments and so on.

But we always read statements such as *came from heaven,
was shaken* and *I will pour out*. These words show so clearly
that all that took place was not an act of man, but of God. It
originated from above and was totally a gift.

The only thing these disciples did was to believe that
God would give what He had promised. They simply
prayed, leaving it up to the Lord how He would do it and
when. They were simply ready in their hearts to receive.

Today, we must not try to depart from the way of the
Bible. We can't *make* something fall upon us that comes from
heaven. We can only ask for it and receive it when it comes.

Don't ever desire to have a cheap, man-made Holy
Spirit substitute, because God has already promised that
He would give us the *real* thing. It is better to have nothing

than to have an imitation that will not do anything for our own walk on earth or for the kingdom of God we are supposed to build.

Signs follow. As with being empowered by the Holy Spirit, so it is with the signs. They are not produced by forcing it through means of excitement or "anointed voices." Jesus said, "And these signs shall *follow* them that believe" (Mark 16:17, kjv). We are not commanded to run after them. They will follow us as we walk in faith.

"You will know them by their fruits" (Matthew 7:16). Actually, this is the greatest proof of truly having been in God's presence. If our encounter with the living God is genuine, it will change our lives entirely. When we are truly touched by the hand of the Lord and experience the depth of His presence, we will not remain the same. It is impossible to meet the Son of God face-to-face and not show any evidence of it in your life later on.

According to the Bible, as in the case of the disciples, the greatest change will be in these areas: love, holiness, boldness and power in witnessing, faithfulness until death and a burden for the lost.

A Pagan Practice

Take a look at the heathen religions around you! How do they worship their gods? Is it not through an endless reciting of prayers, pilgrimages and emotions stirred up by drums, dancing and mantras, until some of them fall into a trance?

Don't you hear repetitious prayers and chanting from

the temples, day and night, accompanied by monotonous drums? All of it is designed to somehow bring a desired result.

Is it really necessary to adopt such practices to serve our God?

God is not our puppet who will perform to the strings we pull! We can't force Him to meet us in a certain prescribed way by performing worship acts. Remember, as the Creator, He is the One who is entitled to make the rules and set the terms, not us. It is utterly selfish and immature to try to bring the old times back by force.

HE IS LORD

God's arm is not too short, He has not grown too old, and He is not too weak to do something new and powerful. Remember, He is life itself, the Creator of all. He is able to call new life into being, touch our lives afresh, send a brand-new revival and change us. It is up to Him to choose a quiet or loud, a joyful or tearful way. There is no need for us to help Him out by re-creating artificial spirituality. It will only hinder His work and produce a harvest of flesh.

Give God a chance. Many times we are so busy working up our old, re-created events that we prevent the Lord from giving us something new or touching us in a fresh way.

SHOULD WE THEN "PLAY DEAD"?

Should we just sit at church and do nothing at all? No, our Savior and Lord is truly worthy of our praise. With all our heart, we must praise Him and lift up His name. We must never think that joyful singing, clapping, raising hands or using instruments is wrong in worshiping the Lord.

But there is a vast difference between that and creating a "Holy Spirit atmosphere" by working up the people. *Stirred-up emotions are not the same as Holy Spirit-touched hearts.* Let us not betray and fool ourselves and the people who have been entrusted to us.

The singing and worship should truly glorify the Lord and at the same time prepare us to meet Him in a new and fresh way.

How to Receive

But how can we receive anything without "working" it up and forcing it to happen?

Jesus clearly gives us the answer in Matthew 7:7–11 and Luke 11:9–13 — *ask, seek* and *knock*. Jesus gives us His best just for the asking!

When we ask, we need to ask in faith, and God expects us to be serious enough about our request that we are willing to wait in His presence until we receive His answer. There is nothing wrong in praying for one another or in waiting upon Him with fasting and prayer.

To prepare our hearts to receive what He already has promised to give, we must be washed by the blood of the Lamb. Our relationship to Him must be unbroken by sin. Our desire must be to belong to Him alone and to serve Him with all our hearts. We must have laid down our lives completely on His altar, holding nothing back from Him. It is a time of total surrender and total submission of everything we have and everything we are. Our whole beings are laid into His hands, to fill with Himself.

When we have given ourselves to Him in this way, we will experience that His grace and His love come and cover us and give us the faith and assurance that He will keep His promises.

Only total surrender creates the kind of faith that will receive.

Maybe you wonder how you can come to such a place of total surrender and faith. That's why the Lord tells us to ask, to seek and to knock. As we do, the Lord reveals the hindrances that are there and helps us remove all of them. He is the One who leads us step-by-step until our hearts are ready and prepared. The day we receive His promise will be a day of great joy and a day of knowing His presence.

Evaluate Your Life and Ministry

Once we have understood a truth, then comes the most painful part of obedience to God: honest evaluation of our life in the light we have received from His Word.

If you are a pastor, Sunday school teacher, elder or Bible woman—may I humbly request you to please think for a moment about your normal worship service, class or group. When you are the leader, teacher or visiting evangelist, what do you usually do?

- Do you encourage your people to re-create past events?

- Do you "work your people up" to a certain level of excitement?

- Do you allow the drums to get louder and louder, the beat faster and faster, until it influences people's heartbeat, breathing and movements?

If you do all these, then the kind of "Holy Spirit" *you* created is nothing else than man-and-drum-powered. This "spirit" then moves according to the volume of your voice and drum. This is opposite to the Bible, which declares: "The wind blows where it wishes and you hear the sound of it, but do not know where it comes from and where it is going; so is every one who is born of the Spirit" (John 3:8).

This verse alone shows us that the Holy Spirit is not controlled by us or our attempts to make Him operate according to the "instruction manual" of our group or denomination.

Please understand me correctly. I don't want to put down you or your church. But my heart aches and is burdened when I see God's people suffering because of the lack of reality in their lives. The Lord wants His people to have the best: true power, true worship and a true experience of His presence. Should traditions, lack of understanding and lack of teaching hinder them the rest of their lives from becoming all God wants them to be?

As I write to you, I, too, have the responsibility to evaluate my life, walk, worship and experience. Some of the things I have shared with you are the result of having walked through a "jungle" of teachings, practices, opinions, persuasions, observations and my own hopes and wishes for re-creation.

As a young Christian, I can remember how torn apart

I felt by so many conflicting teachings and practices from various groups. At that time, I found there were two things that helped me the most:

One, studying the Word of God, discovering exactly what it teaches about the subject, and never departing from or compromising its teaching. Then, judging my desires and experiences by the Word.

Two, comparing my experience with the real thing. Once you have truly met the Lord, you can't forget it. His presence leaves such an imprint in your heart that nothing else compares. You know what is self-made by comparing everything with this imprint. It is neither the outward "form" of how you met the Lord nor your response. It is the depth of the Lord's reality.

HAVE THE COURAGE TO CHANGE

Maybe you never realized how you led God's people in this area. Maybe you just adopted traditions without asking questions. What are you going to do now, after you have looked at it more closely?

This is the hard part. If you are in any kind of leadership position, even if you are just the head of your family, God will hold you responsible for the sheep in your care! You have to answer Him for each of their lives.

If you realize your church or group has a lack of reality and you plan to do nothing about it, then may I ask you this question: "Do you love the Lord so little that you allow such an imitation in His body?"

Have the courage to change. It will not be easy at first.

You must have much patience, clear teaching, wisdom, prayer and *loving* correction. The most important thing is your own example. Look at your life and become a "living instruction." Then you need to teach your wife, family and coworkers. If they don't follow you, your efforts will be greatly weakened and will probably fail.

Also, remember each person is so different in their expressions of joy, sadness, worship and love. God has created all of us unique. He does not expect or command us to express our love to Him in all the same ways and with the same level of intensity. I believe that He enjoys the great variety of children He has. He has given us freedom to celebrate, to praise, to worship and to love Him. *But He wants us to do it with all our heart and absolutely based on the reality of His presence.*

Once your people taste the difference, they will love you and will be thankful to you for leading them from re-creation and imitation to truly knowing Him.

10. CALLED TO OVERCOME

What is God's plan and realistic expectation for our Christian life here on earth? There are a lot of things we could do for Him and many church activities we could get involved in. There are positions we could fill, strategies we could plan and social work we could carry out.

Yet there is one thing God expects from all of us regardless of our different callings: He expects us to overcome!

Overcome what? The world! We read this in 1 John 5:4: "For whatever is born of God overcomes the world."

The "world" sounds so all-inclusive. I believe that is why the Lord chose this word. He literally expects us to overcome everything that approaches us on this earth, for example, the enemy (the devil), opposition, attitudes, anger, persecution, poverty, people—simply everything there is!

Because overcoming the whole "world" sounds too troublesome and too difficult for us, we Christians have cut 95 percent of God's expectations out of our lives. In fact, most of us have narrowed down our goals for over-coming to three or four things — maybe ten — but not more than this.

Let us read 1 John 5:4 again: "For *whatever* is born of God overcomes the world."

This verse tells us clearly that there is not one born-again believer who is exempt — due to circumstances, abilities or lack of education — from overcoming the world! We might as well admit that God never changes His mind on anything. Mark 13:31 says, "Heaven and earth will pass away, but My words will not pass away." Once He makes a requirement for us, it will stand always — whether we live it or not.

SUPPRESSION INSTEAD OF OVERCOMING

We all have memories of times when we overcame and of other times when we didn't.

Some time ago, I talked with a Christian girl who had problems with someone at her workplace. She was trying so hard to have a good attitude, to respond in a Christian way — but she felt quite frustrated. She would do all right for a few days, and then she ended up as discouraged as before. After I talked with her awhile, it dawned on me that this sister was not overcoming the problem but was suppressing it instead.

Suppression might well be the greatest enemy of over-coming, because at a glance, it seems the same or very similar. When we suppress a problem, we "swallow" the symptoms and resolve the situation intelligently. We logically deal with it or explain it away. But deep down it is still there—growing—and some day it will reappear because the final victory has never been won! The battle has been arrested, but only for a while. The problem has been dealt with through retreat, not through victory.

TRUE OVERCOMING

Jesus expects us to overcome. Overcoming is *always* preceded by a battle, a fight—in which we have prevailed and the end result is victory.

Victory doesn't mean that the situation or the person we had difficulty with has changed in our favor. It may have, but I am not talking about this as victory. The real victory is in our heart, not in the circumstance at all. Then we will see results like these:

- The personality of that coworker doesn't bother me anymore

- The constant correction and criticism of my teacher don't create opposition and bitterness in my heart

- The negative attitude of my relatives or neighbors doesn't produce resentment and retaliation

I am now able to respond to these situations with love. I don't feel the pressure and the downward pull as I did before. It is as if I am detached and my heart doesn't receive or store the negative input anymore. When I search my heart, I can't find conflict. I feel at peace, my joy is undisturbed, my response is love; I am even able to bless the one who gives me such a hard time. In other words, I have overcome!

HOW TO OVERCOME

We know now that God expects us to overcome, but *how* is it done? We read in 1 John 5:4, "This is the victory that has overcome the world — *our faith.*"

So the first step to overcoming the world is *through our faith.*

Now I know a number of believers who try to move mountains by their faith. They claim things, command things, speak things into existence and wait for spectacular results. But when we read the next verse carefully, it puts our "faith" in the right perspective: "And who is the one who overcomes the world, but he who believes that Jesus is the Son of God?" (1 John 5:5).

According to this verse, it is not blindly having faith in my faith. It is having my faith *fully* concentrated and centered on Jesus — the Son of God — for whom nothing is impossible.

The book of Revelation gives us a clear illustration about those who overcome: "And they overcame him [the devil, the world — everything] because of the blood of the Lamb and because of th*e word of their testimony,* and they *did not love their life even to death"* (Revelation 12:11).

Let us find out what each of these three statements means in regard to overcoming:

". . . because of the blood of the Lamb": Only through the death of Jesus on the cross and His shed blood can we be

redeemed from the kingdom of darkness to become children of God. With this blood, sin was washed away and can no longer rule over us. Death and the devil were defeated for all eternity. The blood of Jesus not only broke every chain that the devil used to hold us captive, but it is also powerful enough to give us victory in all the battles ahead of us.

"... *because of the word of their testimony"*: This means their public proclamation of putting *their* faith completely in Jesus and His shed blood, accepting His victory as theirs.

Our testimony of salvation, too, is our story of throwing ourselves completely on Jesus by faith. This results in experiencing the power of His blood washing us totally clean.

Our faith will not do anything for us and will not at all enable us to overcome anything if we don't trust Jesus with the same totality as we did at our salvation, believing in Him to bring about the overcoming. *Our* faith standing alone will only amount to suppressing the problem but not overcoming it. It *has* to be our faith *in Jesus,* with the total emphasis on Jesus as the Son of God, who is able to do all things.

"... *they did not love their life even to death"*: This is the most important part of overcoming.

This statement doesn't just mean that these believers happened to be Christians with a martyr mind-set. It simply means that their death was the price of overcoming. They had no reservations about the method God would use to help them overcome, and they had no hidden agenda to tell Him how to work. They did not necessarily expect an easy solution. They were totally willing and content with His way of dealing, as well as with the end result — death!

THE SECRET OF OVERCOMING

"They did not love their life" tells us about these martyrs' humility of heart to accept overcoming *God's way*. It illustrates so beautifully the principle of overcoming and victory.

Jesus overcame the devil by *dying* on the cross. He continually taught that "unless a grain of wheat falls into the earth and dies, it remains by itself alone; but *if* it dies, it bears much fruit" (John 12:24). We find this same principle in these martyrs of Revelation 12:11.

The secret of overcoming is through dying – to die to the right of recognition, honor, position, respect and so on. If I have died to these things, they can't bother me any longer; they can't put pressure on me or make me react resentfully. It won't work anymore, because I am already dead.

The reason it is so hard for us to overcome is because *we fight death*. Somehow, we want to be loved, respected, recognized, understood and treated right. What really hinders us from being *willing* to not love our life "even to death" is our hidden pride. Maybe we are quite humble, but even a flicker of "life" (pride) is enough to keep us from "dying" and thus from overcoming the world.

11. Preparation for Battle

Have you ever wondered why just before a major spiritual event or battle, you are all of a sudden confronted with struggles in your own heart?

You discover bad attitudes, resentment, bitterness, pride, unholiness, lack of patience, lack of love, neglected duties—things you didn't know were there or you thought were mastered long ago.

It seems very disturbing to you to have to deal with these conflicts just before such an important upcoming event.

You did your best to try to shut out all outside disturbance so you could prepare yourself with prayer, fasting, studying, reading books, making plans and raising funds. Now this! Is it the devil disturbing you? Maybe. He is trying to look for ways to hinder God's work every time there is a chance.

But if what comes your way just before a battle has to

do with *your* holiness, *your* attitudes, *your* recognition of failures or sins of *your* own heart and *your* willingness to repent . . . then it is not the devil, but the Lord!

Call to Consecration

Do you know what God's *first* step is to prepare us for battle?

It is *not* the revelation of great strategies and special anointing. They come later. It is *a call to consecrate or cleanse our hearts!*

The Lord knows well that we can't win against the powers of darkness unless our hearts are consecrated and totally His. In order to give us such an opportunity, He has to shine His light very deep into the innermost parts of our hearts. The result: All of a sudden we see ourselves as He sees us, and we feel terrible. In fact, it totally crushes us.

He doesn't do this to make us feel bad or to put us down. No, it is His call to consecration.

Look at the children of Israel when they left Egypt and traveled to their promised land. They faced many battles as well as important encounters with the Holy God Himself. Before some of these major events, the Lord instructed Moses and later Joshua to consecrate the people.

Actually, throughout the Bible God called His people, their kings and their leaders to cleanse, purify, consecrate, separate and sanctify themselves before He could meet them face-to-face, give them victory in battle, provide for their needs, heal their sick, restore their land and accept their offerings.

VICTORY FOLLOWS CONSECRATION

When you read your Bible, watch for these special calls of God. Whenever God laid out this condition and His people responded with cleansing and repentance, God's presence and victory *always* followed as a result.

Let us look at some examples when God's call for consecration of His people preceded a battle, a spiritual encounter or a revival:

Before Jacob made an altar at Bethel

Call: "So Jacob said to his household and to all who were with him, 'Put away the foreign gods which are among you, and purify yourselves, and change your garments' " (Genesis 35:2).

Results: "As they journeyed, there was a great terror upon the cities which were around them, and they did not pursue the sons of Jacob" (Genesis 35:5).

Before Israel was to meet God at Mount Horeb

Call: "The LORD also said to Moses, 'Go to the people and consecrate them today and tomorrow, and let them wash their garments; and let them be ready for the third day, for on the third day the LORD will come down on Mount Sinai in the sight of all the people' " (Exodus 19:10–11).

Results: The Lord spoke to them face-to-face (Deuteronomy 5:4).

God gave them the law (Exodus 20:1–17).

God made a covenant with Israel (Exodus 24:8; Deuteronomy 5:2).

Before Israel crossed the Jordan River

Call: "Then Joshua said to the people, 'Consecrate yourselves, for tomorrow the LORD will do wonders among you' " (Joshua 3:5).

Results: "All Israel crossed on dry ground" (Joshua 3:17).

"Their [enemies'] hearts melted, and there was no spirit in them any longer, because of the sons of Israel" (Joshua 5:1).

Before marching against Jericho

Call: "At that time the LORD said to Joshua, '. . . circumcise again the sons of Israel . . .' " (Joshua 5:2). Circumcision was an outward sign of separation from all other heathen nations, a sign of belonging to God's own possession — the people of Israel.

Results: The captain of the Lord's host met Joshua (Joshua 5:13–15).

Joshua received instructions about how to conquer Jericho (Joshua 6:2–5).

Jericho was taken (Joshua 6:20).

Before sin could be identified and removed from the camp (after losing the battle at Ai)

Call: "Rise up! Consecrate the people . . . O Israel. You cannot stand before your enemies until you have removed the things under the ban from your midst" (Joshua 7:13).

Results: Achan was identified as having sinned and was punished (Joshua 7:18–26).

        Ai was taken and victory was restored (Joshua 8:1–29).

Before a priest or a Levite could serve the Lord

Call: "And also let the priests who come near to the LORD consecrate themselves, lest the LORD break out against them" (Exodus 19:22). It was life-threatening to try to minister before the Lord without total consecration!

Result: The priests and Levites were able to stand before the Lord — accepted and able to serve Him and God's people without fear (Hebrews 9:6).

Before God revealed who would be king in place of Saul

Call: " 'Consecrate yourselves and come with me to the sacrifice.' He also consecrated Jesse and his sons, and invited them to the sacrifice" (1 Samuel 16:5).

Result: God revealed the one He chose as king over His people (1 Samuel 16:12).

Before carrying the ark of the covenant

Call: "Consecrate yourselves both you and your relatives, that you may bring up the ark of the LORD God of Israel, to the place that I have prepared for it" (1 Chronicles 15:12).

Result: With great joy they brought the ark, which was the symbol of God's presence, from an isolated place to Jerusalem, the center of Israel (1 Chronicles 15:25–29).

Before they could cleanse the house of the Lord from idolatry

Call: "Listen to me, O Levites. Consecrate yourselves now, and consecrate the house of the LORD, the God of your fathers, and carry the uncleanness out from the holy place" (2 Chronicles 29:5).

Results: After their own consecration, they were able to clean out every part of the temple (2 Chronicles 29:15–18).

Sacrifice, praise and worship were restored (2 Chronicles 29:21–29).

The people rejoiced, returned to God (revival) and removed idolatry from their land (2 Chronicles 29:36; 30:11–13, 21, 25, 26; 31:1).

NEW TESTAMENT CONSECRATION

There is a continuous call for consecration of God's people throughout the New Testament.

Every time we read words like this in the New Testament—repent, turn from, cleanse, separate, purify, be holy, sanctify, humble yourself, submit—we must recognize that this is a definite call to consecration for the believer. Each of these words describes one of the aspects of consecration.

All these words indicate very definitely and clearly that God's presence, power, deliverance, miracles and answers do not come cheaply or accidentally. They are absolutely conditional. In fact, they are as conditional as in the Old Testament. We talk so much about God's love that we often forget that we serve a holy God. He does not compromise and lower His standards and conditions.

Yet He Himself has provided for us a great advantage over the Old Testament times: He gave us His Spirit to indwell us. His Spirit reveals our need for consecration through the Word of God. Then, along with the Word, He carries out the work of consecration and thus enables us to meet God's conditions. All it takes on our part is obedience.

Please do not misunderstand this to mean that once we meet God's conditions He owes us something. It is not something we work for, and then He is forced to pay us because we earned it. Rather, it is total grace. We will never reach a level of spirituality where we are above grace. It is His grace that saves us and calls us to serve Him . . . His grace that stops us before a battle . . . His grace that shows us our heart . . . His grace that calls us to consecration . . . His grace that makes us willing to submit . . . His grace that accomplishes the work of consecration. It is His grace that enables us to meet His conditions, and it is by His grace that He goes before us in battle.

How Does This New Testament Consecration Happen?

Consider these words: ". . . having cleansed her [the Church] *by the washing of the water with the word"* (Ephesians 5:26). This means that in order to be clean we must allow God to "wash us out" with His water: God's Word. This is where our obedience is required:

- Accept the Word as truth.

- Allow it to reveal what is defiled and what needs cleaning.

- Submit to the washing, scrubbing and brushing until every corner is cleansed.

- Dedicate that cleaned area to the Lord and keep it separated, consecrated and holy for His use only.

Results of New Testament Consecration and Cleansing

". . . that He might present to Himself the church in all her *glory,* having *no spot or wrinkle* or any such thing; but that she should be *holy* and *blameless"* (Ephesians 5:27).

"Now may the God of peace Himself *sanctify you entirely*; and may your spirit and soul and body be preserved *complete, without blame* at the coming of our Lord Jesus Christ" (1 Thessalonians 5:23).

"Therefore, if a man cleanses himself from these things, he will be *a vessel for honor, sanctified, useful* to the Master, prepared for every good work" (2 Timothy 2:21).

After studying these passages, the message to us is very clear: God can only meet us face-to-face or go before us in battle if our hearts are totally clean.

If He sees us approaching a battle or a spiritual encounter and He finds our heart anything less than perfect toward Him, He has to stop us in the midst of our preparations and *first* call us to consecration.

Once our hearts are cleansed, we are in a position where God can work on our behalf. We now will become more than conquerors — through Him.

12. FROM STRENGTH TO STRENGTH

Listening to the testimonies and conversations of my Christian brothers and sisters, I have had the feeling more than once that believers go from problem to problem, from discouragement to discouragement and from failure to failure. This is strangely in contrast to the Bible, which says that God's people go from strength to strength (Psalm 84:7).

IS IT NORMAL TO RUN OUT OF STRENGTH?

Should believers then have no problems, trials or discouragements? No, the Bible says we will have them as long as we live on this earth. Should these Christians put on a smile then and pretend everything is just wonderful? No, that would be living a lie and surely be wrong in the sight of God.

God's Word shows us in many examples that as a Christian encounters problems and trials and lives through them, he is expected not only to be an overcomer, but to end up with *more* courage, with a *stronger* commitment and with *more strength* than he had before. After all, we have received the Spirit of power (2 Timothy 1:7) and the weapons of warfare (2 Corinthians 10:4)!

If we have received all it takes to win the battles, we should now grow stronger with each trial, becoming steadfast in our walk, solid, immovable, an encouragement and example to others and a pillar in the church, able to face any storm.

Instead, it seems for many believers as though each new trial drains more and more strength until they are completely exhausted, unable to stand for themselves and surely not useful for God at all.

You Forgot to Learn Something

If what I am speaking of is your testimony and frequent experience — and you are born again, filled with God's Spirit and not living in any sin — then you have left out something important from the basic foundation of your Christian life.

There are at least three basic things that are absolutely necessary for a newborn baby to survive: to breathe, to eat (drink) and to cry.

Crying makes the baby exercise his lungs. He also kicks his arms and legs while he cries. All this exercise has the purpose of building up enough muscles and strength to one day be able to crawl, sit, stand and walk on his own.

Likewise, the newborn Christian needs the same three basic things for survival: to pray (breathe), to read God's

Word (food to eat) and to learn how to find and develop strength (crying and exercise)! This learning to find strength enables him to live, to face trials and difficulties and to walk with the Lord.

Of course, there are hundreds of other important things a baby, as well as a new Christian, should learn in order to function properly. But some of those who have not learned how to find strength always seem on the verge of dying, and a "church rescue team" has to rush out on emergency calls to try to revive them as they barely hang on to a thread of life. This kind of life-threatening existence is not a healthy one, and it will not encourage unbelievers to trust our Lord.

When we became Christians, our church taught us how to read the Bible, to share our testimony, to sing hymns, to say a public prayer, to attend the services faithfully and to bring an offering. But often no one has ever taught us how to strengthen ourselves in the Lord, especially when we have to go *all alone* through battles.

That would be the same as sending a driver out on a journey with a new car but never telling him how to refuel. After some driving, the engine starts to cough, and then cough some more, and finally it will die for good, leaving the new car and his driver stranded on the roadside. His only hope is now for someone to come along and put some gas in his tank, which will keep him going for a few more miles until the process starts all over again.

Unless and until the driver learns *for himself* where the gas station is and how to refuel his car, this story will become his daily experience.

WHAT DOES IT MEAN TO STRENGTHEN OURSELVES?

To strengthen ourselves as believers means not just to find encouragement. It also means having the ability to continually draw new strength while going through the difficulties of life and ending up with enough strength left to face more. Thus, living from strength to strength will become a reality!

Could you do it? What would you do if your whole church faced a serious problem and all the believers, including the pastor, looked to you for direction, encouragement and strength? Could you give these things to them?

Maybe you would say, "I am not a pastor or elder — I am not qualified for this."

But you are a believer! You have received the same Bible with the same promises and the same Holy Spirit as they did. The problem is not whether you are qualified but if you know how!

David was faced with exactly such a problem. From his experience we can learn three things: *what not to do, what to do,* and *how to do it.*

THE PROBLEM

Please read with me one story from David's life, found in 1 Samuel 30:1-19.

Long before this incident, David had been anointed by Samuel to be the next king of Israel. But at this time in his life, this had not yet come to pass. Even though he had proven himself faithful, Saul was after him to kill him. David and his 600 men were fugitives, hiding everywhere, until they and their families were allowed to live in Ziklag, a city in the country of the Philistines, the enemies of Israel.

One day David and his men returned home only to find their city destroyed — burned up by fire, their possessions carried away and their families taken captive. When they least expected any troubles, their enemies had come and won the victory.

David's story could be your story: All your accomplishments have been wiped out. Sickness has devoured all your savings, you have family problems and everything seems to be falling apart. Maybe you are a Gospel worker and a day came when your church was destroyed by opposition, your coworkers left you and the believers you counted on went back in fear. You are all alone. The work you built up during the past 10 years lays in ruins. Do you know how to find strength to start all over again?

What Not to Do

When David and his men saw the destruction, they were deeply hurt and discouraged. The next thing they did was to come together, not to encourage each other but to weep and to pull each other further down! David, their leader, who usually had such a great trust in the Lord, joined his people in weeping and discouragement.

The Bible says, "The people . . . wept until there was no strength in them to weep" (1 Samuel 30:4). The result was total desperation and complete hopelessness. From this verse we can conclude that before they joined each other in mourning, there was at least a little strength left, but even this was completely drained by the time they got through weeping.

This is exactly what we often do in our homes and churches. Instead of finding ways to strengthen ourselves and others, we get together to "mourn." We tell each other how terrible the situation is, and we agree together that it is going to get worse. In this way, we pull each other further down.

Because of the utter hopelessness his followers felt, David's life was threatened. His most faithful warriors, who at other times were willing to lay down their lives for David, now accused him because they were too desperate to even think and act reasonably. As their leader, he was blamed for everything that had happened. All of a sudden, David was under even greater pressure than the rest of his men. He was reaping the consequences of joining his men in their hopelessness, weeping and desperation.

What to Do

At this point David got ahold of himself, and he remembered what the only hope was for him and his men: to find *new* strength in the Lord. Yet looking at the story, we are almost shocked to find out that David was the only one who had this idea, who seemed to know how to do it and who actually attempted it—one man out of 600, including a priest!

Do you realize how critical David's situation was? Because none of the others knew what to do, all 600 depended totally on David to pull them back out of this valley of despair! Their whole future, their unity, their hope, their victory — even the lives of their captured family members — depended on David's ability to be able to strengthen Himself in the Lord.

When David went to the Lord to receive strength, tremendous pressure and responsibility were on his shoulders: If he failed — all would fail. There was no other man among them who would have attempted this.

How to Do It

"But David strengthened himself in the LORD his God" (1 *Samuel 30:6).* From this verse we can see that David went into God's presence knowing that he was approaching *his* God. It was not the priests' or the elders' or the prophet Samuel's God, but *his own* personal God. David knew God by personal experience and relationship. He had access to His presence, and he was not rejected.

David remembered God's faithfulness, promises and the past victories: the lion, the bear and Goliath. In this particular passage, it doesn't say he remembered, but we know, simply by his coming, that he did. He would not have come to approach his God if he had not remembered all that God had done for him previously. This remembrance gave him *hope*.

When we need strength, it is good to look back on our lives to see how far the Lord has brought us and through how many trials He has already led us.

David waited in God's presence until strength came. We know he waited, because verse 6 says, "But David strengthened himself in the LORD his God." This action is recorded only one time. David didn't go back and forth to try. He went and stayed until he was strengthened before he faced his 600 men again.

He did exactly what Isaiah 40:31 tells us to do: "Yet those who wait for the LORD will gain new strength." The entire emphasis of this promise is on the word "wait":

- *Wait* in His presence

- *Wait* until the answer comes

- *Wait* until the victory is won

- *Wait* for direction

- *Wait* for comfort

- *Wait* for the strength you need

God didn't tell us to wait five minutes and then try something else, to ask your pastor to say a blessing on you, to talk about your problem to everyone at church, or to go from place to place to ask all the evangelists you can find to touch your head and hope for a miracle of strength to fall on you.

The only direction we have received from the Lord to gain strength is to *wait in His presence!*

If you didn't receive strength, then you didn't wait long enough! Prevailing prayer and waiting in His presence are the secret of gaining strength.

If you want to go from strength to strength as the Bible expects you to do, then you have to go from waiting in His presence to waiting in His presence. There is no other way. It is that simple, and it works every time!

THE RESULT

The result of David's ability to strengthen himself in the Lord was incredible.

First, he helped the priest do his job, then he asked and received counsel from God on what to do next. His new strength and courage enabled him to restore unity among his 600 people, to encourage them to trust God again, to pursue the enemy and to fight.

They won the battle and recovered all — nothing was missing. It was a complete victory!

David's ability to strengthen himself in the Lord and then to go out and strengthen others with the same strength he had received was the key to total victory.

Truly knowing God's presence and learning to wait there are absolutely necessary to survive as a Christian!

13. THE PROBLEM IS TOO HARD

Lord, You have allowed many problems in my life, and You have helped me come through them. But this time I think You made a mistake. The problem I am facing is more than I can bear. I wish I had another problem, not this one! Lord, I am breaking under it. My strength is gone. I want to stop hurting, but I can't. I am unable to help myself. With all the faith I have, I have thrown myself on You, but I don't see how I can live through this one.

"LORD, I THINK YOU MADE A MISTAKE"

I was sitting on the floor in my room, feeling like the prophet Elijah after he had run into the wilderness to save his life from Jezebel, who threatened to kill him. He seemed to be even worse off than I was though, because he had added one more sentence to my prayer: "It is enough; now, O LORD, take my life" (1 Kings 19:4).

Reflecting back on my life, I could remember the difficult times when I lost my friend through a fatal accident, when I was falsely accused of lying, when my superior humiliated me in front of others for no reason, when people I trusted turned against me, when people perceived me as deceived and fanatic and when I had given up and walked away from things and people who would cause me to compromise my commitment to the Lord.

All of these were past, and for each of them I had received enough faith and strength from the Lord.

A SPIRITUAL BATTLE

This time, however, the depth of hurting was far deeper than I had ever experienced in my whole life. It took all my energy and strength just to bear up under it for one day. With all my heart I wanted to shake off the problem and overcome, but it seemed as if the problem was glued to me, immovable.

All I was able to do was to desperately cling to the Lord with my whole being. Any solution or victory seemed so far away. For many, many nights I could only sleep a few hours, and for several weeks I could hardly eat anything. Sometimes I would find an excuse to leave the table so I could throw away the food on my plate without anyone seeing it. It just wouldn't go down my throat. I am very seldom sick, and the Lord has given me a strong body, for which I am thankful. But now I felt the battle affecting my body also. I never before had experienced such tiredness and weakness. When I lay down on my bed, I did not have enough strength even to move. For the first time in my entire life, I had to pray for physical strength to get up and make it through the day.

Looking back, I know now that what I faced was surely more than a regular problem. It was an intense spiritual battle! I will not know the extent of it in this life, but I surely could feel the symptoms of it. At this point I knew that the only One who could help me now was the Lord Himself. But so far, I didn't know how He would do it.

He Knows My Frame

While I was telling the Lord that what I was going through was above my strength and that I was afraid He laid more on me than I could bear, He started to speak to my heart. He told me that He knew that I would come through, because He had prepared me for this battle all along. Also, He had evaluated my strength before He allowed the problem to come, and He had found it sufficient, because He was going to give me His.

There in my room, the Lord reminded me of Psalm 139, which I had read many times before. At that moment, however, it became alive in the light of my problem and struggle:

- Verse 16: He knew me and all about me before I was formed. He knew about this battle too.

- Verse 2: He knows my thoughts, including my fears, from afar.

- Verse 5: Long ago, when He called me and saved me, He laid His hand upon my life. He enclosed me behind and before, and He does so even now as I walk through this problem.

- Verse 15: My frame, including the strength it has, is not hidden from Him. Therefore, He knows well how much this frame can bear.

- Verses 9–10: Wherever I go, there His presence will be with me. He even chose to walk with me through this valley of the shadow of death (Psalm 23:4).

- Verses 17–18: In the midst of my problems, He has not forgotten me! His thoughts are precious toward me, even right now. In fact, He thinks so much about me in my struggle that His thoughts outnumber the sand.

I was weeping while the Lord spoke to my heart. Nothing miraculous happened. My problem, and all of the battle, was still there. I was hurting just the same, and I had not received any solutions or instructions.

Yet there was a difference. I was comforted by His love and by the knowledge that the Lord knew my strength and that He was aware of how much I could bear.

STRENGTH TO TRAVEL

In 1 Kings 19:5-8, we read how Elijah was there in the wilderness ready to die. But we also read that in the midst of his problem and despair, God sent an angel to wake him up, give him food to eat and tell him to go to meet the Lord. This happened twice. The food didn't solve Elijah's problem, but it gave him enough strength to travel for 40 days. He was on the way to his solution: Mt. Horeb. Yet before he could reach there, he still had to travel through 40 more days of problems! His strength returned in the presence of God, and there His battle was turned into victory.

I didn't know when my battle would come to an end. But I found that while I was walking through my wilderness toward finding God's presence and victory, He sent me "food" to give me just enough strength to keep on walking.

One such occasion was when He reminded me of Psalm 139. Another one was when some believers came to visit. They didn't know about my battle, but just their presence told me that the Lord had not forgotten me, and He had sent them to walk beside me a little way through my desert. The third time I can remember was when at church I heard a Sunday school girl sing the song, "In the Name of Jesus We Have the Victory." These three things became my "bread and water" to keep me going toward my victory.

When and how would my victory come? Altogether, my struggle must have lasted about 45 days. I wanted so much just to stop hurting, but even though I tried, I couldn't stop it. Neither could I find a solution to my problem. It is hard for me to describe to you how intense this battle was. There was nothing I had faced before with which I could compare it.

During some of those days, I even had a very difficult time praying. My mind would not concentrate on prayer but rather focused continually on my hurt and my problem. I really wanted to fight this battle with prayer, but my strength would crumble while I was on my knees. During these days, the Lord told me, "If you can't pray, read the Word." So I would read and read until my mind was strengthened enough by His Word that I could pray again.

THE BATTLE IS OVER

The day when the Lord gave me victory, I was visiting a home during a series of two Gospel meetings. A sister I love very much was also staying at the same house. I had not seen her for awhile. From the expression on her face, I knew that she had immediately recognized that I was not my "old self." Several times that afternoon she said to me, "Sister, you are hurting so much." I didn't reply. A few times I could see a sad expression on her face when she looked at me.

Just before we had to go to the next meeting, I went to her and asked, "Please pray for me." She took me in her room and closed the door. Then she put her arm around me and prayed with all her heart for me. She didn't know a word of what was troubling me, but she loved me and she must have realized that I was at the end of my strength. When she was praying to the Lord for me, she wept. I can't remember anyone weeping for me before. It seemed that she felt the pain I felt, and she was taking it to the Lord on my behalf.

Nothing spectacular happened while she prayed. But

when she finished praying, I immediately realized that my hurt was gone. I can't explain how, but it was completely wiped away. For the first time in all these weeks, my heart felt light and free from struggle. I distinctly remember almost holding in my breath, as if the hurt would come back any second if I just moved. But it didn't.

For many of the following days, I asked the Lord continually to specifically protect my mind and my heart against any attack. I literally asked Him, "Lord, please place one hand on my mind and the other one on my heart. Don't allow anything to enter my mind or heart that would bring that battle back."

Whatever war had taken place in the unseen world, I don't know. But I knew the battle was over, and it was won after my sister had prayed for me. From that moment on, I could see the victory taking place before my eyes. Not only did the hurt never return, but all the symptoms of my struggle disappeared over a short period of time. In the following days, weeks and months, the Lord worked out every detail of the problem in such a way that I can only praise Him. He filled me with new strength and new courage that can only come from His presence!

Maybe you wonder why I couldn't find the victory by myself, simply seeking and waiting in His presence, which is the normal way to receive new strength.

I don't know. The only explanation I have is this: We can only see a very small part of the war that is taking place in the spiritual world. Sometimes the forces against us are too many, and we are pressed too hard. When that happens, we need reinforcement to outnumber the enemy.

SENT OUT AGAIN

God had picked up Elijah there in the desert for a purpose: first to meet and strengthen him at Mt. Horeb and then to send him out again to work for Him (1 Kings 19:15–18).

The Lord is doing the same with us also. After we have come through our trials, fire, water or desert, He strengthens us for the purpose of sending us out again. We have learned new lessons, and He wants us to use what we have learned to build His kingdom.

Looking back at this problem that was almost too hard for me, I am thankful for what it taught me. No, I would not choose to live through it again. But without it, I would not know:

- How sufficient His grace is, and therefore His strength, in my weakness (2 Corinthians 12:9)

- How He is able to reach deeper than the deepest hurt in my heart

- How He remains faithful to bring me through, even if my faith and strength crumble (2 Timothy 2:13; Philippians 1:6)

- How much power He has to carry me when I am too weak to walk

There is much more the Lord has used from this experience to help me understand, pray for and strengthen others in their trials. In fact, half of this book would not have been written if I had not been allowed to go through this problem. May all our battles result in bringing glory to Jesus!

14. BROKEN FOR A PURPOSE

A doctor can treat an illness only as far as his knowledge of it goes.

An athlete can perform only according to his previous training.

A guide can only show a path or place where he has traveled before.

A teacher can teach only what he himself has studied.

In the same way, a spiritual leader can lead you only to the point he is at himself. Anything beyond this is knowledge borrowed from someone else, theory without practical application and words not yet proven by his own life.

Because of this, Jesus has gone all the way ahead of us to taste every temptation and to experience every kind of suffering a believer could ever encounter. Even more than that, He had to bear all the judgment an unbeliever will face before the living God. "For we do not have a high priest who cannot sympathize with our weaknesses, but one who has been tempted in *all* things *as we are,* yet without sin" (Hebrews 4:15). Here are just some of the things He experienced:

Physical: Hunger

Tiredness

Pain

Poverty

Sickness, as He bore ours

Death

Emotional: Sadness

Accusations

Loneliness

Rejection

Betrayal

Fear (when He prayed in Gethsemane)

Spiritual: Encountering sin wherever He went

Total separation from God as our sin was laid on Him

Experiencing God's wrath toward sinful mankind poured out on Him at the cross

Because of all this, we can be sure that Jesus' understanding of our trials and suffering is complete. His compassion is real, and His ability to teach us what to do in every situation and to guide us through is perfect.

Jesus had to taste it all, not for Himself *but because of us*. He was broken for a purpose: "For since He Himself was tempted in that which He has suffered, He is able to come to the aid of those who are tempted" (Hebrews 2:18).

The same principle applies to us! When we face trials, we too are broken for a purpose. It is not only so that we can learn something new — that too — but so that others will benefit from our experience. How? We are now able to relate to *their* trials, to *their* tears, to *their* suffering and fear. Why? So we can comfort them and help them exactly the same way the Lord comforted and helped us.

Paul writes about this truth in 2 Corinthians 1:3–6:

Blessed be the God and Father of our Lord Jesus Christ, the Father of mercies and God of all comfort; who comforts us in all our affliction so that we may be able to comfort those who are in any affliction with the comfort with which we ourselves are comforted by God. For just as the sufferings of Christ are ours in abundance, so also our comfort is abundant through Christ. But if we are afflicted, it is for your comfort and salvation; or if we are comforted, it is for your comfort, which is effective in the patient enduring of the same sufferings which we also suffer.

From his passage, however, we can clearly conclude one more thing: If we are Gospel workers, our trials will be harder, the tests more difficult and the suffering more intense.

Why? Because we do not lead only one person, but many. We are not only a role model before their eyes, but we must have the ability to go *before* them, knowing where we lead them and where we ask them to follow. We must pass the test before they ever have to attempt it. We must have wept over their hurt before they hurt, so we can comfort them with compassion.

I am reminded of some of our pioneer missionaries who went to places where they encountered tremendous hardship, opposition and suffering. They walked through these trials, and God gave them the grace to stand and to build a church.

Biblical "heroes of faith" also had to experience these hardships, not just to build a church or learn new things about God. They also had to go through these trials because of us. So today I can look at their lives and find courage to obey my own calling. Through their living testimonies, I gain strength to prevail and faith to throw away my life for the Gospel, knowing it will not be in vain. Their faithfulness, their perseverance and their sacrifice have become the sources of my greater trust in the same God.

When one of these brothers and sisters counsel me, their words will not be theory, the tears they weep with me in my trial will be real and their prayers on my behalf will be deep. Why? Because they walked the same road already, long before me.

Over and over we read this phrase in the Bible: "I am

the God of Abraham, Isaac and Jacob." This quote has a purpose not only for God to identify Himself, but it is also a reference and a constant reminder for us of all the things these men experienced with Him in their lifetimes.

They too had been broken for a purpose, along with many others who walked with God ahead of us. The stories of their lives were chosen to be put in print to become examples for us.

In fact, the Bible tells us in 1 Corinthians 10:6 and 10:11 that all that has happened previously is for our example and instruction.

Understanding this principle of being broken for the purpose of serving others helps us find another meaning in the Bible verse that says, "And from everyone who has been given much shall much be required; and to whom they entrusted much, of him they will ask all the more" (Luke 12:48).

As we put this verse alongside 2 Corinthians 1:3-6, it is no longer only a verse indicating our greater accountability for the material or spiritual wealth we possess. Now it also helps us see that the more leadership or influence we have in the kingdom of God, the more suffering will be required on our part in order to be able to fulfill the task correctly.

In our modern days, it has become a deception that a higher position in the Church of the Lord must bring more comfort, more benefits, more cash — and less suffering. Yet when we look closely at the Old and New Testament prophets and leaders, we discover an interesting "hierarchy"! The more God used someone and the higher his position, that much higher and more intense was the level of his suffering and brokenness.

This puts Jesus on top of this hierarchy of suffering, followed by Moses, Paul, the apostles, martyrs and prophets of the Old and New Testaments.

Remember, when you ask God for greater use in His kingdom, you are asking for a greater level of suffering to qualify for the job!

As you go through the trials of your life and have a hard time understanding why, read 2 Corinthians 1:3–6 often, trusting the Lord to give you strength and knowing that this moment you are broken for a purpose.

If this book has been a blessing to you, please
send us a letter in care of the address below.
Thank you.

GFA Books
1800 Golden Trail Court
Carrollton, TX 75010

a division of Gospel for Asia
www.gfa.org

 GOSPEL FOR ASIA

After 2,000 years of Christianity, how can it be that nearly 3 billion people are still unreached with the Gospel? How long must they wait?

This is why Gospel for Asia exists.

More than 20 years ago, God specifically called us to invest our lives to reach the most unreached of the Indian subcontinent through training and sending out native missionaries.

Gospel for Asia (GFA) is a church-planting organization dedicated to reaching the most unreached in the 10/40 Window. Our 14,500 pastors and missionaries serve full-time to plant churches in India, Nepal, China, Bhutan, Myanmar, Sri Lanka, Bangladesh, Laos, Vietnam and Thailand.

Native missionaries are highly effective because they work in their own or a similar culture. They already know, or can easily learn, the language, customs and culture of the people to whom they minister. They don't need visas, and they live economically at the same level as their neighbors. These advantages make them one of the fastest and most effective ways to get the Gospel to the millions who are still waiting to be reached. By God's grace, GFA missionaries have established more than 21,000 churches and mission stations in the past 10 years.*

However, the young, economically weak Asian Church and her missionaries can't do it alone. The enormous task of evangelizing nearly 3 billion people takes the help of the whole Body of Christ worldwide.

That is why GFA offers those who cannot go themselves the opportunity to become senders and prayer partners of native missionaries — together fulfilling the Great Commission and sharing in the eternal harvest of souls.

To find out more information about Gospel for Asia or to receive a free copy of K.P. Yohannan's best-selling book *Revolution in World Missions*, visit our website at www.gfa.org or contact one of our offices near you.

As of 2004

UNITED STATES GFA, 1800 Golden Trail Court, Carrollton, TX 75010
   Toll free: 1-800-946-2742 E-mail: info@gfa.org

AUSTRALIA GFA, P.O. Box 3587, Village Fair, Toowoomba QLD 4350
   07 4630-1580 E-mail: infoaust@gfa.org

CANADA GFA, 245 King St. E., Stoney Creek, ON L8G 1L9
   Toll free: 1-888-946-2742 E-mail: infocanada@gfa.org

GERMANY GFA, Postfach 13 60, 79603 Rheinfelden (Baden)
   07623-797-477 E-mail: infogermany@gfa.org

NEW ZEALAND GFA, P.O. Box 302-580, North Harbour, Auckland 1330
   Toll free: 0508-918-918 E-mail: infonz@gfa.org

SOUTH AFRICA GFA, P.O. Box 28880, Sunridge Park, Port Elizabeth 6008
   041 360 0198 E-mail: infoza@gfa.org

UNITED KINGDOM GFA, FREEPOST NAT11108, P.O. Box 166, York YO10 5ZY
   Freephone: 0800 083 9277 E-mail: infouk@gfa.org

MATERIALS FROM GOSPEL FOR ASIA

AGAINST THE WIND

In this eye-opening book, K.P. Yohannan challenges you to consider how you are running the race God has set before you. Like the apostle Paul, you too can learn what it takes to be able to one day say, "I have fought the good fight; I have finished the race; I have kept the faith" no matter what the obstacles.

(HARDCOVER) *Order ISBN: 1-59589-031-9*

REVOLUTION IN WORLD MISSIONS

In this exciting and fast-moving narrative, K.P. Yohannan shares how God brought him from his remote jungle village to become the founder of Gospel for Asia.

Order ISBN: 1-59589-001-7

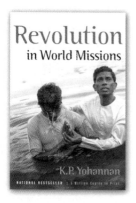

THE ROAD TO REALITY

K.P. Yohannan gives an uncompromising call to live a life of simplicity to fulfill the Great Commission.

Order ISBN: 1-59589-002-5

For more information on Gospel for Asia, visit *www.gfa.org*

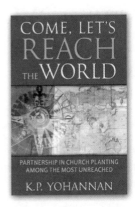

COME, LET'S REACH THE WORLD

How effective are the Church's current missions strategies? Are the unreached hearing the Gospel? K.P. Yohannan examines the traditional approach to missions—its underlying assumptions, history and fruit—in light of Scripture and the changing world scene. This book is a strong plea for the Body of Christ to partner with indigenous missionaries so that the whole world may hear.

Order ISBN: 1-59589-003-3

LIVING IN THE LIGHT OF ETERNITY

K.P. Yohannan lovingly, yet candidly, reminds Christians of their primary role while here on earth: harvesting souls. This book challenges us to look at our heart attitudes, motivation and our impact on eternity.

Order ISBN: 1-59589-004-1

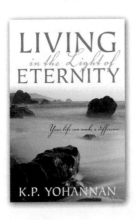

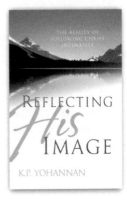

REFLECTING HIS IMAGE

K.P. Yohannan takes us on a journey back to God's original purpose for each of our lives: to reflect His image. This book is a compilation of short, easy-to-read chapters that deal with following Christ closely.

Order ISBN: 1-59589-005-X

For more information on Gospel for Asia, visit *www.gfa.org*

EXCITING DVDs

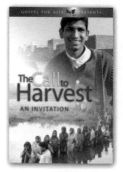

THE CALL TO HARVEST

In this 25-minute DVD, you'll meet the people who are near to the Father's heart: the unreached. See them through the eyes of native missionaries like Titus and Joseph, who face danger and hardship to preach the Gospel in Asia. As the life-giving presence of Jesus transforms lives and families daily, the Lord is calling His people everywhere to come and share the joy of this harvest.

Order ISBN: 1-59589-009-2

CHRIST'S CALL: "FOLLOW MY FOOTSTEPS"

In this compelling 41-minute DVD, K.P. Yohannan challenges us to follow in Christ's footsteps—steps that will deliver us from our self-centeredness and cause us to impact the lost millions in our generation.

Order ISBN: 1-59589-006-8

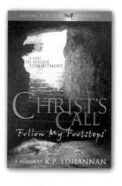

TO LIVE IS CHRIST!

Feel the passion of K.P. Yohannan as he describes the life-giving power of total commitment to Christ in this 55-minute DVD. Be amazed by stories of missionaries who risk their lives to preach the Gospel. Weep with him as he recalls his mother's years of sacrifice that changed lives for eternity. Many people search in vain for the path that leads to the abundant life that Jesus promised. K.P., through the Word of God, uncovers that path in this inspiring and challenging message.

Order ISBN: 1-59589-007-6

For more information on Gospel for Asia, visit *www.gfa.org*

JOURNEY WITH JESUS SERIES

VOLUME ONE

Living by Faith, Not By Sight (56 pp); **Journey with Jesus** (56 pp);
That They All May Be One (56 pp); **Principles in Maintaining a Godly
Organization** (48 pp)

Order ISBN: 1-59589-032-7

VOLUME TWO

A Life of Balance (80 pp); **The Way of True Blessing** (56 pp);
Seeing Him (48 pp); **Dependence Upon the Lord** (48 pp)

Order ISBN: 1-59589-033-5

VOLUME THREE

The Lord's Work Done in the Lord's Way (72 pp); **The Beauty of
Christ through Brokenness** (72 pp); **Learning to Pray** (64 pp);
Stay Encouraged (56 pp)

Order ISBN: 1-59589-034-3

For more information on Gospel for Asia, visit *www.gfa.org*

FREE EMAIL UPDATES

SIGN UP TODAY AT WWW.GFA.ORG

Hear from today's heroes of the mission field.

Have their stories and prayer requests sent straight to your inbox.

GOSPEL FOR ASIA UPDATE   June 10, 2003

116,000 Subscribed   Vol. III Issue 31 — Archives

Moses Makes a Miraculous Escape

Dear Friend in Christ,

Just now we received good news about native missionary Moses, who was kidnapped May 19 by a terrorist group in Bangladesh. On the night of June 9 he escaped after all eight men guarding him fell asleep! Even with his hands tied behind his back, Moses ran through the jungle. He does not know how many hours he ran before he came to a road. Moses kept running until he reached a town the next afternoon. There the Lord provided a safe place where he is now taking refuge until GFA leaders can reach him.

Remember Moses' brother who traveled to talk with the kidnappers? Before Moses escaped, the terrorists found and severely beat the brother and others with him. "Do not return without money," they warned. They threatened to kill Moses if the money was not brought soon. By God's grace, these believers arrived home safely.

Photo of the Week

Archives

Breaking News from Asia

Listen now! Real / Windows
Updated daily two-minute radio clips from Dr. K.P. Yohannan.
Archives

Sponsor a Native Missionary

Link your life with a native missionary sharing Christ with those who have never heard. Become a sponsor today!

- ▸ **Fuel your prayer life with compelling news and photos from the mission field.**

- ▸ **Stay informed with links to important video and audio clips.**

- ▸ **Learn about the latest opportunities to reach the lost world.**

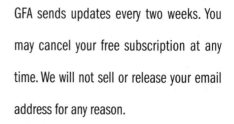

GFA sends updates every two weeks. You may cancel your free subscription at any time. We will not sell or release your email address for any reason.

 **A NATIVE MISSIONARY TODAY!**

I want to help native missionaries reach their own people for Jesus.

I understand that it takes from $90–$180[†] a month to fully support a native missionary, including family support and ministry expenses.

TO BEGIN SPONSORING TODAY,

visit our website at www.gfa.org

or call us in the US at 1-800-WIN-ASIA (1-800-946-2742)
Phone numbers for other national offices listed on page 151.

or fill out the form below and mail to the nearest GFA office.
National office addresses listed on page 151.

❏ Starting now, I will prayerfully help support _____ native missionaries at $30[††] each per month = $_____ a month.

You'll receive a photo and testimony of each native missionary you help sponsor.

❏ Please send me more information about how to help sponsor a native missionary, including a one-year FREE subscription to *SEND!*—the voice of native missions.

Please circle: Mr. Mrs. Miss Rev.

Name _____

Address _____

City _____ State/PR/County _____ Zip/PC _____

Country _____ Phone (_____) _____

E-mail _____

❏ Please send me free e-mail updates.   **HA59-RBPS   ZHV9-RBPS   YHV9-RBPS   3HV9-RBPS**

A higher standard.
A higher purpose.

Gospel for Asia sends 100 percent of your missionary support to the mission field. Nothing is taken out for administrative expenses. All donations are tax deductible as allowed by law.

[†] AUS $120–$200, CAN $90–$180, €45–€60, CHF 80–110, NZ $120–$200, UK £60–£110

[††] AUS $40, CAN $30, GER €30, CHF 60, NZ $40, UK £20

FREE subscription

FOR YOU AND YOUR FRIENDS

Stay informed! Sign yourself, your relatives and Christian friends up for a FREE one-year subscription to *SEND!*, Gospel for Asia's quarterly magazine, featuring exciting and prayer-inspiring stories and updates from our native missionaries working in Asia. Simply fill out the form below for your free subscription.

Please circle: Mr. Mrs. Miss Rev.

Name _____

Address _____

City _____ State/PR/County _____ Zip/PC _____

Country _____ Phone (___) _____

E-mail _____

Please circle: Mr. Mrs. Miss Rev.

Name _____

Address _____

City _____ State/PR/County _____ Zip/PC _____

Country _____ Phone (___) _____

E-mail _____

HA59-PBPH ZHV9-PBPH YHV9-PBPH 3HV9-PBPH

Include additional names on a separate sheet of paper.

❑ Please identify me as the gift subscription donor.

My name is: _____

MAIL THIS FORM to one of Gospel for Asia's national offices listed on page 151.